INFORMATION SKILLS AND THE
SECONDARY CURRICULUM:
SOME PRACTICAL APPROACHES

British Library Cataloguing in Publication Data

Howard, Julie
 Information skills and the secondary curriculum: some practical
 approaches.– (Library and information research report ISSN
 0263–1709 v. 84)
 1. Schools. Curriculum. Information retrieval
 I. Title II. Series
 025.524

 ISBN 0–7123–3255–3

Library and Information Research Reports are published by the British
Library Research and Development Department and distributed by
the British Library Publications Sales Unit, Boston Spa, Wetherby,
West Yorkshire LS23 7BQ. In the USA they are distributed by the
American Library Association, 50 East Union Street, Chicago, Illinois
60611. In Japan they are distributed by Kinokuniya Co Ltd, PO Box
55, Chitose, Tokyo 156. In India, Burma, Pakistan, Nepal, Bangladesh
and Sri Lanka they are distributed by Arnold Publishers (India)
Private Ltd, AB/9 First Floor, Safdarjang Enclave, New Delhi 110029.

RDD/G/868

The opinions expressed in this report are those of the author and not
necessarily those of the British Library.

Typeset and printed in Great Britain at the University Press,
Cambridge.

INFORMATION SKILLS AND THE
SECONDARY CURRICULUM:
SOME PRACTICAL APPROACHES

Julie Howard

Library and Information Research Report 84

Abstract

This report examines the integration of information skills into the secondary curriculum. Although the research focused on the GCSE initiative, it takes a broader view to encompass the implications of the National Curriculum and current developments in the educational scene. The report begins by reviewing current literature on information skills. This draws out the main issues in provision and highlights strategies which could be used at school and Local Education Authority (LEA) levels. The data from questionnaire surveys to each LEA and schools library service in England and Wales are summarised and lead to case-studies of interesting practice in information skills at school or LEA level. The implications for progression, primary/secondary liaison, teaching/learning styles and in-service training are highlighted. The research draws upon current knowledge on the process of educational change and effective in-service training. The report illustrates how schools can implement information skills, and gives examples of effective in-service training and teaching/learning strategies. Finally the report draws together conclusions and recommendations for those working at school and LEA levels.

Julie Howard taught History in Norfolk before joining the Cambridge Institute of Education as a researcher in 1986. She has spent her time there on various TVEI-related research and evaluation projects and on the Support for Innovation Project which supported teachers and schools across Norfolk and Suffolk in their staff development activities. She has recently worked with the team evaluating the National Schoolteacher Appraisal Pilot scheme. Currently she is working on a Training Agency-sponsored Management Development Project and also a DES-funded investigation into patterns of employment and development amongst teachers who have undertaken "long courses" in education. This is the third report she has written for the British Library, the other two being *Information Skills in TVEI and the Role of the Librarian* and *Crossing the Great Divide*.

For my father

Acknowledgements

This project was made possible through the many people in schools library services and Local Education Authorities (LEAs) who gave of their time to fill in the questionnaires and take part in interviews associated with this project. They pointed us in the direction of schools and staff who were willing to open their doors to us. Particular thanks are due to Betty, Liz, Jean, Margaret, Mary, Norma, Petra, Shirley and Sue who gave their time and shared their experience and expertise, and also to Jenny and the many staff of her school who shared their thoughts and classrooms and made us feel welcome and a part of the school throughout many visits and interviews.

Colleagues at the Cambridge Institute of Education provided support and encouragement. Karen Brookfield at the British Library gave continuing support and assistance. Sharon Markless shared our enthusiasm and gave inspiration both to us and to many of the schools and LEAs with which we worked.

In writing this report, I am particularly grateful to David Hopkins, the Project Director, for his guidance throughout the project and advice during the writing stage. He also contributed the first chapter of the report. Above all, I would like to acknowledge the efforts of Pam Carroll who provided administrative support and kept an air of calm and good humour throughout, and Angie Ashton who provided the secretarial support which transformed the manuscript into a work of art.

Finally, though I am indebted to all the above for their contributions and am sure any merit this report has is due to them, I should point out that the weaknesses and omissions are entirely my own.

Contents

Introduction

This is a report of a project, based at the Cambridge Institute of Education and funded by the British Library Research and Development Department from 1989 to 1990, on "Information Skills in GCSE and the Role of the Librarian". The project was directed by Dr David Hopkins, the research was carried out by Julie Howard, and Pam Carroll provided administrative support.

Towards the end of the project the data indicated that school librarians would welcome research on their professional development needs. They were feeling overloaded by the number and complexity of the various national initiatives, such as the Technical and Vocational Education Initiative (TVEI) and the General Certificate of Secondary Education (GCSE) and currently the National Curriculum, to which they were expected to respond. The British Library consequently funded a short-term research project on "The In-Service Training Needs of Chartered School Librarians" (Howard and Hopkins 1990). This led to the extension of the "Information Skills in GCSE and the Role of the Librarian" project, with its completion date extended to November rather than September 1990.

The British Library also funded a complementary project "Information Skills, Library Use and GCSE" based at the Centre for Educational Development, Appraisal and Research (CEDAR), University of Warwick (1989-1991) and directed by Professor Robert Burgess with research being carried out by Dr Helen Phtiaka. During the period of overlap of funding for the two projects, i.e. September 1989 to November 1990, the two project teams have worked together sharing findings and perceptions. Joint dissemination conferences were planned for summer 1991.

In order further to disseminate the project's findings, we have organised two separate two-day information skills workshops for librarians together with a teacher from their school. A similar one-day workshop for advisers and schools library service (SLS) representatives has been organised further to disseminate the idea of working in partnership.

Rationale

The stated educational objectives of the GCSE are to improve the quality of education and to raise attainment standards across the

1

ability range. The GCSE criteria which lay down assessment objectives have a similar content for each subject. They call for each pupil in each subject, to learn how to learn, how to use what they have learnt and how to communicate this to others. Pupils are required to be able to use books and other human and media resources to define a problem, select the facts they require, analyse them, look at alternative solutions, evaluate their chosen solution and present it. In other words there is a universal requirement for pupils to have highly developed information skills.

Previous initiatives such as TVEI and Certificate of Pre-Vocational Education (CPVE) similarly called for highly developed information skills. The librarian's professional expertise including working with teachers in planning courses, providing suitable resources, sharing in the development of students' reading skills, liaising with external agencies, and his or her expertise with research and information skills can enhance pupils' learning. Therefore the librarian's role in the curriculum is vital.

Our previous research on "Information Skills in TVEI and the Role of the Librarian" presented a somewhat gloomy picture with school librarians being isolated, and the poor networking of good practice in information skills teaching. During the course of the TVEI research, however, we saw evidence that the advent of GCSE was changing the picture. There appeared to be a greater understanding of information skills and the role of the librarian in the curriculum of the school. Funding was sought from a number of bodies and this process delayed the start of the project by three years, to 1989. By this time students had sat GCSE examinations and the National Curriculum was on the educational horizon. We were unsuccessful in gaining funding from these other bodies and we were delighted therefore when the British Library decided to fund our research on "Information Skills in GCSE and the Role of the Librarian".

The Project

During the project we gathered information on the extent of information skills teaching in GCSE and the role of the school librarians in this provision. Data-gathering methods included a telephone questionnaire (see Appendix 1) survey of SLS provision in each Local Education Authority (LEA) in England and Wales and to the Chief Adviser in each LEA. Data from this enabled us to identify site visits that included SLS personnel, schools and advisers. More detailed data-gathering strategies included interviews, classroom/library observations and the collection of documents pertaining to GCSE and information skills in the school/LEA. The LEA visits included those to two metropolitan district councils, a Welsh LEA and four shire counties.

In addition to our approaches to LEAs and SLS we asked what provision each GCSE Examination Board in England and Wales had made for the handling of information skills in their GCSE training. However, by 1989 most Examination Boards were well into the implementation phase of GCSE and it has proved difficult to access information regarding training strategies which had taken place some four years earlier. However, the recent reports by Her Majesty's Inspectors (HMI), published by the Department of Education and Science (DES), on GCSE discuss the links with Examination Boards and in-service training, and we turn to those for information (DES 1988a, 1988b, 1988c, 1990a, 1990b).

Our nationwide survey of information skills provision in GCSE produced a low response rate (33% SLS and 13% LEAs). There appear to be a number of reasons for this disappointing questionnaire return rate, apart from the usual problems of questionnaire design. GCSE had been *in situ* for some three years by the time the project began. It was not therefore possible to pinpoint one particular person in an LEA who was responsible for its implementation, as responsibility for GCSE had by then been dispersed across the advisory service. GCSE was losing its central position in people's minds as the implications of the Education Reform Act of 1988 were beginning to take hold in LEAs and schools. It was therefore just one of several important curriculum initiatives.

At the present time LEAs, SLS and schools are busy grappling with the implications of the National Curriculum, Local Management of Schools (LMS), open enrolment and governor involvement. In addition several colleagues within the SLS spoke of the number of questionnaires which they were being asked to complete. The LEAs were also under pressure from the quantity of questionnaires they were receiving from individual research students and institutions. For example, one Principal Adviser quoted two questionnaires per week, which if answered would take up six hours of his time. Despite the lack of statistical data which could have been drawn from a larger response rate the questionnaires were invaluable in providing documentary evidence outlined in Chapter 1 and in highlighting schools and LEAs for further visits.

As stated in our previous report *Information Skills in TVEI and the*

Role of the Librarian (Howard and Hopkins 1988) and reiterated by Peggy Heeks in her survey of the information skills movement (Heeks 1989) the dissemination of educational research is problematic; one reason being the style, language and level of detail used. In reporting on this project we have therefore attempted to be brief, accessible in style and to focus on key issues. The audience for this report is the practitioner, i.e. teachers and librarians working at classroom and LEA levels.

The Report

In this report we first review the recent literature on information skills. The purpose of the review is to draw out the main issues in the provision of information skills and the strategies which could be used at school and LEA level.

The project findings draw upon the responses to a questionnaire circulated to Advisers and SLS personnel. In order to maintain confidentiality we have deliberately anonymised responses. Where quotations have been taken from questionnaire responses they have therefore been recorded as (SLS Q), or (LEA Q) for the Adviser responses. However, several respondents stated that their LEA had been involved in various research and development activities related to GCSE and/or information skills. They kindly sent us copies of published research or other comments connected to this. Where such material has been published and thus available to a wider audience those documents have been acknowledged in the text.

Similarly, the schools and LEAs visited during the course of the project have been anonymised and the personnel have been given fictitious names. There is a dilemma here in that interesting practice is to be celebrated and disseminated as widely as possible. On the other hand institutions have to be protected from visits and enquiries from vast numbers of interested outsiders. We are very conscious of the demands made upon schools, LEAs and the SLS in these times of rapid change, and have therefore decided upon the policy of anonymising. This had been agreed with the schools concerned.

The work carried out by schools, LEAs and the SLS reflects the situation at the time of the fieldwork. As such it marks a stage in their development and therefore should be viewed as part of an ongoing process which continues to develop. School visits ranged in number from one to a dozen per school, thus the work we reflect can only be seen as a snapshot of the work that is being undertaken.

During the course of our research schools began to take on the implications of the National Curriculum. In some schools this led them to name their year groups according to the National Curriculum Council guidelines. In other words children in secondary schools traditionally known as first years became known as Year 7, seconds as Year 8, thirds Year 9, whilst fourth years became known as Year 10 and so forth. However, the HMI reports we refer to generally use the traditional terms. In this report we refer to the age groups in the way that our sources of data recorded them, and there is therefore a mixture of traditional and modern.

Given the advent of the National Curriculum, with its emphasis on skills, we have deliberately addressed this report to a wider brief than the one we set out with. The strategies and advice set out in the report apply equally to the implementation of the National Curriculum. It is therefore relevant to all teaching and learning in secondary schools. Similarly, there are strategies for liaison between primary and secondary schools which might be helpful to our primary colleagues.

In preparing this report we have tried to build upon existing knowledge. At the same time we highlight successful strategies and issues for further development as seen in the schools and LEAs we visited. In order to help readers develop their approaches to information skills we have expanded some examples to show "cameos" of what such strategies look like in practice.

In Chapter 1 we review the surveys of provision and advice on strategies from recent research on information skills. We draw out the main conclusions for the implementation of an information skills programme in schools.

Chapter 2 examines the findings from the documentary evidence gained from our questionnaire surveys, from HMI reports and GCSE specific reports. We look at the implications of the National Criteria and Assessment Objectives, and GCSE coursework and assignments for teaching/learning styles and progression. In the light of these implications we examine the early in-service support from Examination Boards and LEAs and discuss the findings of recent research on effective in-service education and training.

Chapter 3 examines how some of our case-study schools began work towards a whole-school approach to information skills. We use a background of implementation theory then move towards "cameos" or brief outlines of examples from schools. We then look briefly at other initiatives which might be used to facilitate such an approach, namely school development plans and LMS.

Chapter 4 examines examples of school-based in-service education and training. In this section we detail some of the strategies used by the individual schools or LEAs. There are detailed outlines here which other schools may find helpful in drawing up their own strategies.

Chapter 5 looks at learning strategies at the classroom level. In this section we use "cameos" to describe the work we found in some of the schools we visited.

Finally we draw some conclusions and make recommendations for action.

1 A Review of Surveys of Provision on Information Skills and Advice on Strategies

For the purposes of this review, the information skills movement can be divided into surveys of provision and advice on strategies. In what follows, these two aspects of the literature are briefly reviewed, and some guidelines deduced.

Surveys of Provision

The Library and Information Services Council (LISC) published its report in 1984. The summary of the report suggests:

> Firstly that school libraries and school library services have a vital role to play in educating children to be able to make use of information in formal education and throughout life. Secondly that school libraries are underused and thirdly that they are underfunded.
>
> (LISC 1984)

The LISC report continues to argue:

> that the school library has an essential and central task in the school curriculum and that library skills are its foundation. This concept has been little discussed in the United Kingdom where, because libraries have been under-resourced, arguments have tended to centre on resource requirements of libraries rather than on the concept of their role in the educational process. If it is accepted, as the report argues, that a school should have a whole school curriculum policy on information skills underlying all other aspects of curriculum planning, then underuse of school libraries would only occur if libraries were unable to meet users' needs.
>
> (LISC 1984)

The report makes a number of recommendations to a variety of bodies. A selection of those for LEAs, heads and teachers are quoted below.

For LEAs:

> 13.3.1 To clarify the objectives of school libraries and the school library service and to establish a policy framework for them (10.6).

13.3.2   To make adequate financial provision for the stock of school libraries (8.14.2).

13.3.4   To designate specialist posts of Adviser and Inspector for school libraries and school library services (8.11.6) and to ensure that an adequate liaison framework exists for the school library service (8.11.7).

13.3.5   To ensure that teacher librarians and librarians have adequate time to carry out their duties (8.4.3) and to make an effective contribution to the curriculum through a suitable organisational structure within schools (8.6.2, 8.8).

13.3.7   To seek to employ dually qualified staff to work as school librarians (8.7.2) and to employ Chartered Librarians as school librarians where dually qualified staff are not available.

13.3.8   To improve the in-service training opportunities for teacher-librarians, librarians, and all teachers (8.6.4, 8.15.1).

13.3.11   To urgently consider the implications of information technology for information-skills teaching and for the staffing and resourcing of school libraries (8.15.2).

For headteachers:

13.7.1   To take the lead in establishing a whole-school curriculum policy on information skills (7.13).

13.7.2   To give support to their staff who seek to make the school library effective (8.8) and to ensure that they have adequate resources including non-teaching time to carry out their duties.

13.7.3   To consider opportunities to improve the accommodation for libraries which may arise due to falling rolls (8.12.1).

For teachers and librarians:

13.8.1   To be involved in all curriculum matters which concern the library (7.12).

13.8.2   To involve colleagues in a team effort to plan the use of the library and help children to acquire the necessary study skills (7.12).

13.8.3   To devise a programme of library-user education integrated with the curriculum (7.12).

(LISC 1984)

A similar report was published in 1985 in Scotland following the establishing of a working party in 1982 "to consider the resources, implications of the changing curricula and to present guidelines on how School Library Services could best respond to the needs of education". It too produced a list of recommendations which are similar in tone and aspiration to the LISC report. Some of these are:

6.6   The Headteacher should establish a management structure within which the School Librarian will share in resource responsibility with Senior Management and through which positive timetabling for all Departments' use of the School Library Resource Centre is achieved (2.15; 2.17; 2.47).

6.7   The concept of the School Library Resource Centre should be accepted (5.17-5.18).

6.8   Teacher and Librarian should collaborate in a programme of information skills. The teaching of problem-solving skills should be extended from classroom-based worksheets to the School Library Resource Centre. Such work should take account of developments in Information Technology (1.14; 3.18; 2.17; 2.39; 2.47; 3.18; 4.3-4.8).

(LISC (Scotland) 1985)

In 1984 HMI carried out a survey of secondary school libraries in six LEAs. Their conclusions and comments reinforce those of the LISC and Scottish Library Association reports.

Their general conclusion was:

1.3   The survey revealed considerable diversity of provision and use, between LEAs and within the same LEA. With some exceptions, the overall impression was of many libraries which were inadequately staffed and stocked, poorly financed and underused.

9

They also commented on the difficulties involved in setting up an information skills programme:

> 7.8 The more important study of information skills are of course more complex than the simpler issue of imparting basic library skills discussed above. This small enquiry revealed a good deal of interest in them but comparatively little actual practice. Some schools did provide self-contained courses but these were often unrelated to the work the pupils were doing. A number of them realising that these courses were not having the results they had hoped for, were planning new approaches based on the pupils' work in various subject areas. A few schools had set up working parties to discuss these important developments; others were interested but somewhat uncertain of what to do and would have welcomed guidance throughout school, area or subject-based in-service programmes.

The need for a library policy was central to their conclusions:

> 8.2 Perhaps the most important step a school can take to improve its library is the fundamental one of formulating a policy for the library, based upon discussions by the whole staff and presented within the context of discussion about the curriculum. This policy should set out the place and purpose of the library in the school and its various roles. Such a policy document will need to consider the range of resources and services to be provided together with the nature and level of staffing, finance and organisation required to make them available. Above all, it should be concerned with ways of encouraging and developing wider and more effective use of the library by departments and individuals and should include a statement about departmental responsibilities and involvement in the library and its use, with other requirements that this be worked out in greater detail in schemes of work. Finally it should set out a development plan for the next few years. Several schools were moving towards the formulation of a policy but only two had so far produced an embryonic document of this type and were attempting to implement it.

(DES 1985)

Our own previous research project "Information Skills in TVEI and the Role of the Librarian" produced results along the same lines as the LISC, HMI and Scottish reports. It suggested that few teachers appeared to be able to facilitate or appreciate the process of teaching information skills, and that librarians themselves were not systematically involved in TVEI or curriculum development in their schools.

Peggy Heeks in her review of the information skills movement 1983-1988 (Heeks 1989) highlights not only the lack of clarity about the term "information skills" but also the division between the fields of education and librarianship. This division begins at government level where the DES has responsibility for school libraries whilst the Office of Arts and Libraries is responsible for most of the SLS which support school libraries. This divide often continues at local government level where the SLS is separate from the Education Service. It is therefore unsurprising that such a division is still apparent at the school level.

However, this divide is gradually becoming crossed at local government level as the implications of the Reform Act become more apparent. During the course of our GCSE research we found a number of local authorities redefining the role of the SLS and absorbing it into the advisory/inspection sector. Similarly Heeks (1990) finds that:

> The good news is that inter-departmental liaison on School Library Service matters is improving, coming through both in questionnaire returns and on visits.

Though she states that:

> several chief librarians put relations with Education Departments as their main problem.
>
> (Heeks 1990)

Our TVEI findings (Howard and Hopkins 1989) also noted a lack of networking and dissemination of good practice; the pockets of exemplary practice that we had identified were not linked to each other or to the wider environment and there appeared to be no system for so doing. However, the British Library funded the Information Skills in Schools (INSIS) project based at the National Foundation for Educational Research (NFER) from 1985 to 1989 to form a network and disseminate good practice. The project collected resources from schools and LEAs and made them available to those who so requested. The Information Skills Liaison Officer, Sharon Markless, led in-service training sessions in schools and LEAs throughout the country. However, with the ending of the project it is to existing support services within schools and LEAs that teachers and librarians must now turn.

Taken together these surveys present a picture of school library provision and information skills teaching which is patchy, *ad hoc* and underfunded. They are also relatively consistent in the recommendations, of which a coherent library policy appears paramount. It is not the product itself which is of such importance, but the process by which the school draws up the policy. In other words it is the discussion between all members of staff, across subject boundaries, about the role of the library and librarian in the school curriculum.

Strategies

Besides the specific recommendations for good practice suggested by, for example, the LISC report, the literature also contains more detailed advice on how to proceed.

A working group set up by the British Library and the Schools Council and led by Michael Marland, investigated the development of information skills. The group published a report edited by Marland (1981) which was distributed to all secondary schools in England and Wales. In *Information Skills in the Secondary Curriculum*, Marland takes as the guiding theme that in the completion of an assignment, whether it be a PhD thesis or a primary school project, certain kinds of question tend to recur, because certain stages of enquiry have to be worked through in virtually all study activities. Consequently a school's information skills curriculum is outlined in terms of nine questions:

WHAT DO I NEED TO DO?
No project can begin until the pupil has grasped the nature and range of the assignment. Frequently the bald assignment needs extensive refining and expanding.

WHERE COULD I GO?
Depending on circumstances, the time available, the amount of detail required and their own personal knowledge, the pupils have to decide which sources of information are suitable and accessible.

HOW DO I GET THE INFORMATION?
The pupils' understanding of how information is organized, and their skill in applying this understanding, will determine how effective the search is.

WHICH RESOURCES SHALL I USE?
Rejecting resources which are inappropriate is crucial. Those selected must be examined according to criteria determined by the answers to the first question ("What do I need to do?"), and by the pupils' judgement of the right degree of detail, the likely accuracy, and the lack of bias.

HOW SHALL I USE THE RESOURCES?
This is the most important stage, involving a range of strategies determined by the nature of the assignment and the nature of the resources.

WHAT SHOULD I MAKE A RECORD OF?
Deciding *what* should be recorded is very difficult, but it is more important than deciding *how* to record it. Pupils may develop their own methods of recording and filing information.

HAVE I GOT THE INFORMATION I NEED?
At this stage pupils have to interpret and assess the information in the light of the first question, and perhaps repeat certain stages.

HOW SHOULD I PRESENT IT?
Before it can be presented, the information will need to be reorganized into a form determined by the nature of the assignment. Part of the teacher's task here may be to develop an awareness of the range of possibilities open to the pupil.

WHAT HAVE I ACHIEVED?
Evaluation should involve the pupil, other pupils and teachers, and can usefully be undertaken at any stage of the assignment. Any evaluation should be put to good use in the development of strategies for the future.

(Marland (ed) 1981: 24,25)

These question steps were intended as a starting point. Norman Beswick (1988) states that:

the National Guidelines for GCSE include very specific (and for some teachers very revolutionary) elements of skills learning. And prominent among these clearly articulated skills are the skills of reading, writing and number, the skills of accurate transcription and description, of accessing information, assessing its value, using and transforming information, and its assimilation into something original and new: vital skills for a world in headlong change.

(Beswick 1988)

He argues that although they looked at some of these skills in the working party on information skills (Marland (ed) 1981) the list of nine steps was only a beginning, for:

so far as research into how children learn is concerned the Nine Steps have no standing. You could call them an educated guess; and they certainly were not meant to be applied as a universal panacea.

Beswick believes that the GCSE with its emphasis on skills may encourage teachers to:

explore, more thoroughly and sensitively than we had room for in a sixty-page pamphlet, what skills are characteristic of particular kinds of learning and particular types of investigation, and the wide-ranging, divergent and creative ways in which children construct their own valid meaning from the assorted elements they find.

(Beswick 1988)

Similarly the National Council for Educational Technology (NCET) in its 1990 Summary Sheet listed the steps pupils need to take in information handling, the skills and concepts teachers must develop and the areas of the National Curriculum which justify and promote such activity in schools. An example from English, levels 1-3, is for pupils to be able to "refer to information books, dictionaries, word books or simple data on computers as a matter of course. Pupils should be encouraged to formulate the questions they need to answer by using such resources" (National Curriculum Council (NCC)). In Science also they are expected to cover the range of information skills outlined in Marland's nine steps, e.g. "to use secondary sources of information" (Science levels 2-10) "... the interpretation of data, and evaluation against the demands of the problem" (Science levels 2-5). Other examples can be found in the recent report on Geography where they state pupils should:

*   collect relevant information from a variety of sources, for example from visitors, observations and surveys, pictures and photographs, videos, TV and radio programmes, books, artefacts, computer programs; ...

* interpret their findings and use a variety of means to present them to teachers, other pupils and adults, for example, using narrative, tape recordings, writing drama and role play, graphs, maps and plans, 3D models, pictures and IT; ...

(NCC 1990)

Geography students are expected to use a range of primary and secondary sources of information. They are expected to evaluate and present their work. The examples we have just given are but extracts from the National Curriculum; there are of course, many more statements relevant to information skills. As with GCSE, the need for information skills is widespread and across most subject areas.

Taking a wider perspective, Markless (1986) has identified and was supporting, in her role as liaison officer for INSIS, four alternative models for the development of information skills in schools. These are:

(1) *School-based approach.* Sometimes a school motivated by the interest of the head or deputy will try to develop a whole-school policy on information skills. Such a policy will be translated into practice gradually over a period of years. In other circumstances the impetus may come from an individual teacher or a department or from the librarian. It may spread outwards influencing others who see the effectiveness of integrating information skills into the curriculum or practice may remain patchy.

(2) *LEA working group.* This is often led by an adviser and involves members from different schools within the authority. Stage one is usually the producton of a policy document on study and information skills, followed up by a discussion and some INSET. The policy usually addresses specific stages of education, for example, primary, eleven to sixteen, and so on.

(3) *Teachers' group* – based on researchers or a teachers' centre. A group of teachers from across the age and subject range are encouraged to meet, to discuss information skills. They often undertake a long-term commitment and during that time discuss problems and develop new strategies and resources with the support of a researcher/teachers' centre team.

(4) *LEA-course based.* Initiatives and money in areas like CPVE, TVEI and TRIST have led LEAs to develop new in-service courses, some of which focus on resource-based learning, problem solving and developing learning skills. Such provision stimulates interest in the information skills area and work on information skills is developed with the support of the LEA, through co-ordinators and secondment. Outcomes of such curriculum development are ongoing with initial INSET courses followed by school-based or consortium-based work.

(Markless 1986)

Tabberer (1987) has developed, on the basis of extensive research, a series of teacher-based strategies for integrating information skills into the curriculum. He describes these strategies:

This project has included a programme of in-service activities designed to help schools seeking to adopt a more carefully planned study and information skills approach. In a sense, the particular activities enclosed in that programme are less important than the idea of the programme itself. *All schools, all departments, all teachers should be examining practice carefully, continuously and, as far as possible, systematically in order to assess a curriculum's qualities and weaknesses.*

This can be done quite easily by means of simple exercises of "pupil pursuits", survey (of homework marking, writing or reading, for example), and observation, which do not necessarily take excessive amounts of additional time and resources. The activity sustains the pressure of continual improvement. It can provide a professional pressure, in a sense, by keeping pupils' learning clearly in focus and constantly alerting teachers to educational needs at a time when many external, administrative demands are competing and, occasionally, threatening to overwhelm professional planning. With a greater sense of pupil difficulty and behaviour, it becomes easier to articulate educational needs to others, easier, for example, to explain and justify to parents certain (otherwise difficult) decisions about their children.

School (and other educational) management has a responsibility to create the climate for this. Time and resources will need to be available for staff to sustain their inquiries. Moreover, those willing to experiment and investigate will require protection from doubters and cynics who too quickly judge on the basis of, say, how much is written neatly and how much noise comes from a particular class. Those taking some risk deserve to be rewarded, not over-criticized. Furthermore, there has to be an expectation that it will take time to make any substantial improvement.

Here is an interesting parallel. The role that seems to be emerging for the teacher in the classroom, as a careful and protective manager of the orchestrated research and exploration by pupils, turns out to be the very role for educational managers. It is not necessary to construct an alternative theory for ways that teachers can learn in the environment of the school; they can learn with the support and the opportunity that they might equally give their classes.

Finally, it is important to stress: *this is not a lonely movement.* It has shared aims with those concerned with active learning (and often with active tutorial work), with resource-based learning, with language-across-the-curriculum, and with many other developments within the subject areas. It is unsurprising that there is such common ground when the issues raised by information and study skills are so broadly educational. The concern within this movement, as with many others which have so many different names, is with the ways pupils learn and the ways teachers, and managers, can best support that learning.

(Tabberer 1987)

In our previous research – *Information Skills in TVEI and the Role of the Librarian* (Howard and Hopkins 1988) – we found that although there were examples of exemplary work in information skills provision, they were isolated, uncoordinated events that occurred as a consequence of individual teacher, librarian, department, school or LEA initiative. They were rarely the result of coherent systematic attempts at cross-curricular innovation. We found that there was a general lack of appreciation of the concept of information skills and that the ideas were not integrated into a predominantly subject-based curriculum.

Secondary schools rarely had an infrastructure to accommodate information skills. Cross-curricular initiatives are difficult to implement given the traditional organisation and curriculum of most secondary schools. Where such an infrastructure did exist it was usually supported by clear direction from the senior management team, by the provision of a clear model to most teachers and departments, a highly visible and well used library or resource centre, collaboration within and between departments and ongoing in-service training to support the required changes in teaching style. We set out a number of guidelines for those working at central, LEA and school levels:

School Level

- establish a cross-curricular commitment to and policy for Information Skills;

- use the library as a central resource for information;

- make use of the librarians' study skills expertise;

- transcend the use of technological hardware; put learning at the heart of TVEI;

- structure in time during the school year for teachers to talk to each other about cross-curricular developments such as information skills;

- use school focused INSET as a means of creating an expertise in pupil-centred learning (as related to Information Skills and TVEI) and sustain it through the use of teacher collaboration and coaching;

- regard the various change initiatives that are currently bombarding us as opportunities for professional development; look for the common threads (usually teaching style) and react to them collectively rather than individually.

LEA Level

- establish an LEA policy for Information/Study Skills;

- integrate the SLS into the advisory service; do not regard it as a "bolt-on extra";

- provide support through advisers, teacher centres and advisory teachers for cross-curricular initiatives;

- establish and sustain networks between schools that focus on exemplary practice and build up a directory of such practices so that schools do not have to re-invent the wheel;

- so arrange the GRIST/INSET programme that a substantial proportion of it is committed to the acquisition and development of teaching skills;

- encourage advisers/inspectors to assume an innovation perspective.

TVEI Coordinators

- transcend the use of technological hardware; put learning at the heart of TVEI;

- promote skill specific INSET on teaching styles that utilises specific teaching strategies and an integrated presentation/modelling/practice/feedback/coaching INSET design;

- encourage cross-curricular initiatives;

- prepare TVEI staff to become experts in Information/Study Skills, teaching strategies and coaching; use them to initiate a training the trainers approach;

- create and sustain networks between schools and establish a directory of exemplary practices.

MSC [later the Training Agency and more recently the Training Enterprise and Education Department]

- provide more clarity at the outset about the nature of the change required;

- remember that innovation never succeeds as a "bolt-on extra" but needs to be integrated into the rhythm of the school and the LEA;

- understand that change at the local level is about individual learning and that teachers require technical and psychological support at the early stages of any change;

- accept the idea that change takes place over time and that successful change involves a combination of pressure and support; but it is collegial pressure through interaction with other teachers, advisers, co-ordinators etc who are working together within a collaborative and supportive environment.

(Howard and Hopkins 1988)

The literature reviewed seems to suggest the importance of a whole-school policy for information skills. Such a policy is, however, difficult for schools to implement. There are a number of reasons for this. Firstly, any cross-curricular policy is difficult given the traditional subject structure of most secondary schools.

Secondly, it is a complex innovation requiring attention to the change process. There needs to be active initiation. At this stage the innovation needs to be clearly articulated and we have already noted the confusion and lack of clarity about the term "information skills". There needs to be an active advocate, and there has to be in-service education and training to support teachers and librarians. During the implementation phase information skills have to be well coordinated, have adequate and continuing internal and external support, and have control increasingly spread throughout the school. Those involved in the implementation need rewards such as supply cover, shelter from other demands (difficult in such times of rapid change and increasing demands such as responding to the Educational Reform Act) and positive feedback. During the institutionalisation phase of the innovation, information skills will need to be embedded in the school organisation, tied into classroom practice, have widespread use in the school and LEA and be supported by continuing in-service education and training.

Thirdly, as Paul Lincoln points out:

There is also a natural suspicion of any talk of whole school policies. It is often based on the fear that a policy will be rigid and restrictive and will not allow the variety of styles and the freedom of approach that has been regarded as a strength of the curriculum, in this country.

(Lincoln 1987)

He argues that a whole-school approach is desirable because that allows room for the teacher's individual "style". Policy statements have neatly tied ends yet the learning process is not that simple or tidy. He describes essential ingredients for a whole-school approach to learning:

(a) It must develop from where teachers are and not be imposed upon them;

(b) it must respect the fact that teachers are individuals with their own classroom "style";

(c) it should be descriptive rather than prescriptive;

(d) it should be expressed in terms of practical classroom techniques and strategies, so that teachers can see the relevance of it to their own work.

(Lincoln 1987)

Summary

We have chosen these examples of recent development work, not only because they are illustrative of the best advice that we have currently available, but also because they focus their advice at different levels, i.e. the school, the LEA and the classroom.

The literature just reviewed suggests a series of guidelines for the effective implementation of an information skills/library programme within a school. We have summarised this information as follows:

1. Establish a policy/approach at LEA, school and department level.

2. Engage in systematic planning for the implementation of a policy/approach at each level.

3. Provide effective leadership at each level.

4. Provide in-service education and training that utilises a variety of training formats at each level.

5. Try to ensure adequate resourcing (both time and money) at each level.

6. Integrate developments into the curriculum.

7. Involve as many staff as possible in the development and have them collaborate as much as possible.

8. Remember that these developments potentially involve radical

21

changes in curriculum and learning styles and all that that implies.

9. Involve the school librarian at each stage in curriculum planning, in-service activities and curriculum development.

It is essential that students develop information skills to fulfil the requirements of both GCSE and the National Curriculum.

2 Information Skills in GCSE, the Project Findings

With this as background, we now move forward to the findings of the current project "Information Skills in GCSE and the Role of the Librarian". We begin with a general overview of GCSE, looking at the National Criteria and Assessment Objectives, their link with information skills and the role of the libraries and librarians, and similarly GCSE coursework and assignments. We then look at the implications for teaching/learning styles and for progression, the incremental development of information skills throughout the student's school life.

Given the necessary changes in teaching style required throughout the school, which cross both subject and age barriers, teachers and school librarians need ongoing in-service support. We therefore report on some of the in-service education and training for GCSE provided by Examination Boards, the SLS and LEAs. We continue by exploring what is effective in-service education and training by looking at the findings of current researchers in this field.

In this section we examine and discuss the documentary evidence available from relevant DES/HMI reports, previous research and from the contributions made by LEA and SLS respondents to the questionnaire survey.

The GCSE National Criteria and Assessment Objectives

The Secretary of State has laid down criteria which provide a framework to govern all GCSE work. They define the subject, the objectives, content of the course and the areas of knowledge, skills and understanding which students will be expected to demonstrate. Guidelines on the assessment of students are also given. GCSE Assessment Objectives should be central to the teaching and assessment of pupils. They define the skills and abilities pupils are expected to achieve. Teaching and examining methods have to be designed in order to give pupils the opportunities to develop and demonstrate their abilities.

Helen Pain-Lewins and her colleagues (1989) analysed the syllabuses from four GCSE Examination Boards across 16 subject areas. Their findings reflect the need both for resources and for students to have highly developed information skills. They compiled a matrix which clearly shows the type of information skills required of each subject and for each Examination Board (see Diagram 1).

Diagram 1

Summary of information skills specified in syllabuses

	1	2	3	4	5	6	7	8
Biology	ms	m	ms	m wn	ms n	mswn	m n	msw
Chemistry	m		ms n	msw	s	mswn	ms n	msw
Commerce	sw	swn	swn	mswn	swn	sw	s n	mswn
CDT	mswn	mswn	mswn	mswn		mswn	mswn	swn
Economics	swn	mswn	mswn	mswn	sw		m w	m wn
English	n		msw	m n	s	msw	mswn	mswn
English Literature			n	n				
French	w		n	w		n		
Geography	ms n	mswn	mswn	mswn	msn	mswn	mswn	mswn
History	w	mswn	mswn	mswn	mswn	mn	mswn	mswn
Home Economics	m wn	ms n	mswn	mswn	s n	m n	mswn	m n
Mathematics	m			m wn	ms	m n		m wn
Music		s		n	s	s		s
Physical Education		n	wn	wn	w	n	n	n
Physics	m		mswn	wn	mswn	m w	mswn	ms n
Religious Studies	w	s	m wn	s		w	m w	mswn

This is a summary, therefore the subject name covers all syllabuses in that subject.

Key m = Midlands   s = Southern   w = Welsh   n = Northern

1. Identification of problem
2. Location of materials
3. Extraction of information
4. Analysis, interpretation of information

5. Comparison of sources
6. Organisation, recording of information
7. Evaluation, reasoned judgements
8. Presentation of information

(Pain-Lewins et al 1989)

Their report details the information skills needs as stated in each of the 16 chosen subject aims and assessment objectives.

Similarly the Library Association in its *General Certificate of Secondary Education: Guidance Note on the Role of Libraries and Librarians* (1988) gives brief examples of the information skills called for in GCSE assessment objectives in the National Criteria. It cites:

Craft design and technology

Gather, order and assess the information relevant to the solution of practical/technological problems.

English

Evaluate information in reading material and in other media, and select what is relevant to specific purposes.

Geography

Use a range of source materials, including maps at a variety of scales, photographs and simple statistical data.

Demonstrate an ability to select, use and communicate information and conclusions effectively.

History

To recall, evaluate and select knowledge relevant to the context and to deploy it in a clear and coherent form.

Home Economics

To recall, seek out, select, record and apply knowledge relevant to the needs and factors identified.

Science

Extract from available information data relevant to a particular context.

Social Science

Develop the capacity for the critical evaluation of different types of information. The ability to collect, analyse and interpret data.

In each of these cases, and in others not listed, the ability to make proper use of the resources in a library will be essential if the students are to fulfil these objectives.

(Library Association 1988)

In order to support both students and teachers Helen Pain-Lewins further argues in her report that:

There are significant indications that the school librarian

has an important, central role to play and that the professional skills of librarianship could be identified as vital in supporting pupils and teachers involved in GCSE studies.

(Pain-Lewins et al 1989)

In all of the syllabuses analysed by the research team, there was significant weighting given to coursework, enquiry, investigation or practical work.

A number of SLS respondents to our questionnaire indicated that they too had been actively promoting the need for libraries and librarians to have a central role in GCSE in the light of the stated Criteria and Assessment Objectives. A number of SLS reported that they had conducted their own school-wide or LEA-wide research into this area.

For example Kent County Library Services produced a research and development report on the implications of GCSE for the public library service in Kent entitled *He Obviously Had No Idea What He Was Doing*. In the autumn of 1988 its research team conducted a survey across secondary schools in three of its six Education Areas to discover teachers' perceptions of their resource needs for GCSE. The subject areas covered were Geography, English and History. They sent each head of department taking part in the survey background material on the role of libraries in relation to GCSE, namely the Library Association guidance notes, 1988 (see above), and Helen Pain's "Project work & GCSE: can public libraries meet the challenge?" (1988). The team also surveyed public libraries to determine the number and range of GCSE enquiries over a seven-week period in the autumn term.

Their results, like those of Helen Pain-Lewins et al (1989), indicated a wide range of resource needs. In addition:

Teachers indicated that there were formal programmes of information/study skills and/or library skills training in some schools, although it was obvious that the level of provision varied tremendously across the county.

And further:

3.1.13   Teachers indicated that training was most needed in the following areas:

Information skills   41%

Use of reference materials   27%

Effective use of public libraries   22%

(Batt and Sage 1990)

The strain that the demands of GCSE were putting on the public library service was an issue which came up often during the course of our research, although it is beyond the remit of our investigation. However, there are implications for teachers and students. The Kent team's discussions with public libraries raised the following issues:

3.3.1 Problems experienced in dealing with GCSE enquiries highlighted a vital need for training in the following areas:

- for library staff in dealing with GCSE enquiries and teenagers in general;

- for teachers to be aware of the range of services available and how to use the Library Service most effectively. Librarians complained especially of the short notice given of GCSE assignments;

- for teachers to be more aware of available resources. Librarians often had to deal with numbers of pupils researching "impossible" projects, e.g. "find out about the history of insurance in 19th century Ashford" for which no resources appear to exist. If the teacher had checked with the library when planning this work it would have saved many people considerable time and energy;

- for pupils to acquire library and information handling skills, and to have confidence in using the Library Service.

(Batt and Sage 1990)

Other SLS which responded to our questionnaire highlighted similar issues. That is, GCSE criteria and assessment objectives call for a wide range and large number of resources, that these resources have a widespread cross-curricular use and a central base is needed, and that students and teachers need help with research and information skills. Furthermore, there need to be closer links between schools and public libraries.

In the Cambridgeshire County Council publication *Provision of Learning Resources in Secondary Schools* Margaret Smith and her colleagues state:

Though some schools have developed library resource

centres and have made them central elements in their curriculum, many schools have not. Many local authorities, governors, headteachers and staff have not identified the valuable role which well organised resource provision can play. They have a limited view of what a school library can be, and through serious under-funding and under-staffing, its potential has been almost completely ignored. Partly as a result of this, many resources are located in subject departments and the opportunity has not been taken to make the library a central element of a combined resource centre for the benefit of the whole school community.

(Smith et al (eds) 1988)

They go on to say that:

A library resource centre will increase in importance as greater emphasis is placed on assignments, projects and problem solving skills. If student-centred learning is considered to be important, then students will need to be taught how to use resources efficiently and effectively to complete essential coursework. Mixed ability teaching, individualised learning and the increasing need for teachers to keep abreast with new developments places further emphasis on the importance of the library resource centre.

(Smith et al (eds) 1988)

In order to support their staff they have drawn up guidelines for good practice. In addition they have produced a number of subject-specific guides with examples of good practice, resource needs and implications for teaching style (e.g. *Learning Now. The Cambridgeshire Experience in Science* 1990).

The National Criteria and Assessment Objectives explicitly state the need for students to have sophisticated information skills. The new examination system will require schools to have access to a wide range of resources to meet these needs. A central resource, the school library, will need to be available to students. Similarly students will be turning to public libraries to give support and resources. Teachers and librarians will have to work together to build up the skills all students need in order to fulfil the requirements of GCSE, whatever the subject they may choose to take.

GCSE Coursework and Assignments

Students undertaking GCSE have to produce written or practical pieces of work based on their own research and individual study.

Unlike its predecessor the Certificate of Secondary Education (CSE), the coursework of GCSE is undertaken by *all* students across the ability range. Every GCSE student should be able to demonstrate positive achievements through their work. Differentiation or different levels of achievement among students of differing abilities is a feature of GCSE and this is difficult to measure by written examinations alone. As the Education Minister, Bob Dunn, said in his address to employers on 21 July 1987:

> The idea of coursework assessment is to test those skills and abilities which cannot easily be demonstrated in timed, written exams – skills such as the ability to work diligently over a long period of time, to use initiative, to use resources effectively, to work in a team. I don't know about you but that list sounds to me like a fair start to a list of essential management skills.
>
> (Dunn 1987)

Information or learning skills are essential for every subject. Although the more practical subjects give a higher priority to problem-solving, students are expected to conduct a considerable amount of information-searching. The linguistic and literary subjects, such as English, English Literature and French are more concerned with students' abilities to analyse and interpret their materials. Students are expected to select many of the coursework topics themselves from within their general subject area.

This greatly increased amount of individual coursework is placing great pressure on teachers and librarians, as well as the students themselves. Teachers and librarians have to respond to providing materials and information and to teach students sophisticated information skills. In their explanation of their choice of title *He Obviously Had No Idea What He Was Doing* the authors of the Kent research report neatly define the main problem faced by students, teachers and librarians:

> It seems to encapsulate all that can go wrong with GCSE projects and why there is a need for research of this kind. The enquirer had a set task, but only formed in the vaguest terms, the library had some of the information he required but not all, and he did not have the necessary skills to interpret the information he was given in order to synthesise his findings into a coherent whole.
>
> (Batt and Sage 1990)

This hits at the very root of the problem, for as one of our SLS respondents states:

> Information skills cannot be acquired by osmosis and need to be taught in a structured way by every teacher of every subject, preferably in the context of an individual pupil's course of study.
>
> (SLS Q)

The information skills required of pupils for their coursework need to be built up and developed during the course of their classwork. In their report HMI (DES 1988c) point out that:

> The distinction between coursework and other examination work does not essentially lie in the nature of the task or the way it is taught but in the fact that it is separately assessed... In many lessons, it was not possible to tell whether the tasks set were to be separately assessed as coursework or not. This was encouraging as assessed coursework was never intended to be something clearly distinct from other classwork. However since coursework needs to meet particular assessment objectives, teachers are encouraged to set tasks that require pupils to use their initiative to apply a range of skills including study skills, and to plan their work so as to meet deadlines.
>
> (DES 1988c)

Students, then, need a clear framework of skills to support them in their GCSE work. These skills need to be taught in a structured way by every teacher in every subject. Furthermore these skills and teaching/learning approaches cannot take place suddenly in Year 10 or 11, they need to be integral to the learning process at an early age, built upon and developed.

Teaching/Learning Styles

The full implementation of the GCSE therefore requires very substantial changes in teaching and learning styles if these information skills are to be developed in students. This has implications for the whole school and the whole curriculum. Although GCSE has highlighted this need, previous initiatives such as TVEI began work in the same area, as our earlier research (Howard and Hopkins 1988) indicated. We have already argued that the current initiative, the National Curriculum, is similarly requiring widespread use of information skills. One of our SLS respondents noted:

Work done within the extension of TVEI, as part of the development of IT across the curriculum, and now the skills elements within the National Curriculum are all combining to create a climate within which the skills elements are beginning to be understood. Teachers are beginning to extend and modify their teaching styles in order to allow pupils' learning styles to develop... progress is slow because the techniques of managing this sort of change are not yet well developed in schools.

(SLS Q)

The early subject-specific GCSE training did little to encourage cross-curricular skills or to develop different teaching/learning styles. The main focus appeared to be subject content. However, the later GCSE training was seen by HMI (DES 1988c) as "better focused and more effective INSET". They continue:

Sessions have generally been better planned and organised, more informative and effectively presented. Increased time has been devoted to activities and participation and less to formal lectures, facilitating better understanding of the rationale and procedures of the GCSE.

(DES 1988c)

They cite a simulation exercise in a GCSE Music in-service training course which:

proved to be very effective, highlighting teachers' own weaknesses in working together and raising their awareness of some of the problems encountered by pupils when engaged in group activities.

(DES 1988c)

Thus they highlight the need for a range of in-service training strategies and for "modelling the message" that trainers are trying to deliver.

They conclude their report with a number of issues for the future, and teaching/learning remains one of several:

153. Issues for urgent consideration and action
Teaching and Learning: making improved provision for the less and more able; reducing the excessive workload on pupils and teachers; improving the planning and organisation of coursework...

154. Important but longer term issues

Teaching and Learning: increasing the range and variety of teaching approaches and improving differentiation; improving opportunities for pupils to develop study skills...

(DES 1988c)

One of the respondents to the Adviser questionnaire pointed out work that they had undertaken in their LEA in collaboration with others. This was the GCSE Network Project of the London Boroughs of Bexley, Kingston, Merton and Richmond and the Associated Examining Board which produced its research report, *GCSE: A Positive Experience* (GCSE Network Project 1989). This project represented a partnership between teachers, advisory teachers, inspectors and the examining group. It found that GCSE was having a great impact on pedagogy:

> Many teachers referred to a greater relevance as teaching styles and learning strategies have become more appropriate to pupils' interests, experience and abilities. They welcomed the opportunity to introduce more investigative and practical work and to adopt a more thoughtful approach to problem solving. GCSE has often encouraged a less formal style of teaching, involving a more dynamic and enthusiastic approach with a greater variety of teaching methods...

> Teachers noted many strategies that had been encouraged by GCSE. These included:

> – a shift to a wider range of teaching and learning strategies across the curriculum. The teachers were taking on roles as facilitators, and problem-solving approaches, research and active learning were being promoted;

> – clarification of aims and objectives for students and making students responsible for their own learning...

> – the development of study skills, group work and resource based learning early in the school.
> (GCSE Network Project 1989)

They go on to say that there is the need for:

> more widespread provision of INSET on such aspects of teaching as experiential learning and the teacher's role as facilitator.
> (GCSE Network Project 1989)

Teachers talk of the need for ongoing support for their implementation of different, more student-centred teaching/learning styles. We discuss some strategies for this at a later stage in the report. The ability to learn how to learn does not just happen. It is a steady development and therefore students will need to begin at an early age.

Progression

These changes in teaching/learning style will need to take place lower down the school than Year 10 as students cannot be expected to change learning style part way through their school career. As one of our SLS questionnaire respondents states:

> In Inspections and Reviews, I have found that a most important and largely unaddressed issue is that of *progression* i.e. that the need for pupils to have effective information handling skills revealed by GCSE needs to be dealt with *before* pupils embark on GCSE courses.
>
> (SLS Q)

This statement was reinforced in the 1988 HMI report on the introduction of the GCSE in schools, 1986-1988.

> The evidence from both schools and Public Libraries indicates that many pupils lack suitably developed library and information skills when they begin their GCSE courses. Some teachers however are overcoming this by building skills development into their courses, particularly in Years 1-3.
>
> (DES 1988c)

The HMI reports indicate that schools have begun to prepare students for GCSE in the earlier years of secondary schooling. We found one school, for example, which had carried out its own research on GCSE from 1986 to 1988 and recommended that:

> Study skills and resource-based learning appropriate to GCSE should be properly defined and taught throughout the school from the beginning of the intake year.

and that:

> The content and methodology of GCSE should lead to a revision of 1st, 2nd and 3rd year courses and syllabuses. In

future students should not sense an abrupt transition in work-method and expectation between the 3rd and 4th years.

(Olive School 1988 unpublished report for
staff and parents)

There is a strong argument here for a whole-school approach to information skills. Whilst secondary schools experience problems in implementing a whole-school approach, the issue of progression becomes even more problematic at the transition from feeder to secondary and from secondary to sixth form or further education. These issues are highlighted in the HMI report on the GCSE in schools and sixth form colleges. For example, it states:

> Whilst some departments have changed A-level syllabuses in response to the GCSE, far fewer have extended their range of teaching approaches to match the greater variety of styles now used with younger pupils. As a result, teaching sometimes fails to capitalise sufficiently on the many new strengths which students bring to their A-level work. Although students are often better equipped for independent study and research, have a greater range of practical skills, are generally more willing to participate in discussion and group activities, and have better attitudes to problem-solving and investigative work, such activities sometimes remain unexploited as ways of supporting and improving the quality of learning.

(DES 1990b)

In the same way that institutions at 16+ do not always capitalise on students' independent study and research skills, secondary schools do not build on expertise children have developed in primary schools. The large number of feeder primary schools (or middle schools) does not make the task easier for the secondary school, but some children come with highly developed information skills which could be built upon and enhanced. The advent of the National Curriculum may make better liaison between these schools more of a priority. In Chapter 3 we examine in more detail the progress of one secondary school which is working closely with its primary feeder schools.

In-service Support

In order to provide support for teachers during such a complex change, in-service education and training is required. Teachers were being asked to accept a new examination system with all that entailed in changes to teaching/learning style. We know from research (e.g. Fullan 1982, 1985) that change is:

– a process not an event and takes place over time;

– characterised by anxiety and uncertainty particularly in the initial stages and therefore ongoing support is vital;

and that:

– the learning of new skills is incremental and developmental, i.e. teachers need practice and feedback throughout the implementation;

– organisational factors within the school such as the ethos, or leadership style affect the success or otherwise of an innovation;

– support from outside the school, e.g. the LEA/SLS advisory services or consultants, make it more or less likely that GCSE/information skills will succeed;

– successful change involves pressure and support.

When GCSE was introduced there was extensive in-service education and training using the "cascade" model. In other words a member of each subject staff, usually the head of department, was taken out of school for GCSE training and then went back into school to disseminate information. Many teachers felt that this system was inadequate. Criticisms teachers had of early GCSE training included:

– if the "trained" head of department left the school who could train the rest of the department?

– too many teachers out of school, thus disrupting pupils' teaching time;

– difficulty in recruiting suitably qualified supply teachers;

– GCSE implementation clashed with Phase One of TVEI Extension thus increasing teacher absences;

– some course leaders did not have credibility or training experience;

– courses and activities did not build on their experience and

35

teaching skills, and so their confidence in dealing with GCSE teaching approaches was undermined.

However, where LEA courses were delivered by advisers or advisory teachers with knowledge of the schools and where provision was ongoing, teachers were able to discuss classroom practice. In other cases where the leadership and organisation of the Head of Department was strong, there was a successful path towards GCSE implementation.

Teachers felt that they needed:

– ongoing support;

– feedback from moderators to "see how we have done";

– practical rather than philosophical help;

– assistance with assessment procedures;

– help with the new teaching methods.

The report by DES/HMI, *GCSE: An Interim Report* (DES 1988b), outlined the nature and effectiveness of the first three phases of "cascade" training. They found Phase 4 received a mixed reception from teachers:

> For some the experience was useful; in one LEA a local survey revealed that 80% of teachers had found it helpful, but in most areas teachers were less impressed. They criticised the lack of expertise of trainers, and the failure to tackle important issues like coursework assessment in sufficient depth.
>
> (DES 1988b)

By 1988, however, they found that in-service education and training was becoming better focused and more effective and teachers appeared to be benefiting from this.

A number of LEAs/SLS which responded to our GCSE project's questionnaires indicated that they provided in-service support for teachers and librarians. Examples of such in-service education and training activities included:

a) Training for pairs of teachers (deputy head if possible

and teacher in charge of the school library) on a weekend course "The Information Skills Curriculum". This aimed to raise awareness, action planning for in-school development and approximately 75% of the secondary schools attended in 1987...

This in-service education and training strategy is powerful in that one of the senior management team was involved. It is useful to have someone "with clout" involved in the innovation. Also pairs or groups of teachers/librarians from one school give each participant mutual support at the school level. A second course run by this same LEA was:

b) resource-based learning – day course for those teachers who wish to bring Resource Based Learning/Project/ Information Skills type working and groupwork, into their classroom and who generally wish to produce more active, skills based learning for their pupils.

(LEA Q)

This latter course was supplemented by a half day off timetable to plan a module of work. This module was to include the use of a wide range of resources, including those from the school library and the SLS. Further classroom support was provided, and course members met for another half day for group discussion, and evaluation. The Curriculum Development Teacher for Resource Based Learning planned the course and exhorted the school's senior management team to liaise with school library staff in order to target colleagues for the course. Research has shown (Joyce and Showers 1988) that supporting teachers in their own classrooms is a most powerful and effective method of in-service education and training if we want to effect real change in classroom practice.

Other examples of in-service education and training include those where the SLS has worked together with subject advisers. One SLS/ LEA organised a Home Economics and Learning Resources course, as part of an overall in-service education and training strategy, in 1986, which included:

– current developments in Home Economics;

– resources to support developments;

– research skills:

1. GCSE and the School Library:
   How do we set problems?
   How do pupils access information?
   How do pupils analyse/discard/use information?

   What are the investigative skills necessary?
   What was easy to do?
   What was difficult to do?
   Where do pupils need support?
   Who can help?

2. Partnership approaches.

                                                        (SLS Q)

The course leaders included SLS staff, the LEA Home Economics Adviser and school librarians, thus the library and education services were strongly interlinked. In addition to these subject-orientated courses the SLS worked with the TVEI unit to produce a Learning Skills day conference which focused on Learning Skills – a whole-school approach? When do you start? and primary/secondary links. This looked at the issue right across the age range from nursery upwards.

These strategies, though only a snapshot of the work going on nationwide, do indicate successful attempts at partnership between SLS and the Advisory Services, and between teachers and librarians on an LEA-wide scale.

It may be worth exploring in a little more detail here what we mean by effective in-service strategies. For a broad definition of the term "in-service education and training" we turn to Ray Bolam:

> Those education and training activities engaged in by primary and secondary schoolteachers and heads, following their initial professional certification, and intended mainly or exclusively to improve their professional knowledge, skills and attitudes in order that they can educate children more effectively.
>
> (Bolam 1982)

This broad definition takes in all types of courses and puts the improved education of children as the ultimate aim of teachers' in-service education and training, with improved teacher knowledge, skills and attitudes as an immediate aim.

We now have a body of knowledge from research and development studies (e.g. Rudduck 1981, Bailey 1987 and Wallace 1988) which suggest the following necessities for the design and implementation of good training courses:

- collaborative planning involving course leaders, LEA sponsors and former or prospective participants;

- a clear focus upon participants' current and future needs;

- careful preparatory briefing for participants several weeks ahead of the course, with opportunities for pre-course work where appropriate;

- a programme which is structured but has enough flexibility to allow for modifications in the light of monitoring and formative evaluation;

- a programme which is oriented towards experience, practice and action, and using as appropriate, methods like action learning, action research, performance feedback and on-the-job assistance;

- "sandwich" timetable including course-based and job-based experiences to facilitate this approach;

- careful de-briefing after the course and sustained support, ideally including on-the-job assistance where new skills are being implemented.

(Bolam 1987)

Linking courses to individual teachers, schools and LEA needs, in our case information skills, is a crucial point. Who identifies these needs is another. One of our questionnaire respondents described a course set up on "Helping 13-16 year olds with GCSE coursework" in 1989, which had to be cancelled through lack of teachers' support. The subject of this course was clearly of importance to teachers struggling to implement GCSE but they did not recognise it as such. One of the criticisms of external courses is that by their nature they are bound to offer information and experience which is very general and therefore not related sufficiently to teachers' or librarians' specific needs and concerns. Theory has to be closely linked to practice and this is more difficult away from the school, classroom or library.

The Local Education Authority Training Grants Scheme (LEATGS) outlined in Circular 6/86 (DES 1986) also focused on identifying and matching needs, ensuring there was continuing support for the participants and that the training was translated into action. Furthermore, that the in-service education and training should be monitored and evaluated:

– assessing the need of teachers for training including the ways in which the teacher, the school and LEA were involved;

– seeking to ensure that training needs were matched by suitable provision;

– ensuring that the training provided was part of a continuing process of professional development of the teachers concerned;

– ensuring that training was followed up and translated into effective action at the appropriate level;

– monitoring in-service education and training and evaluating its effectiveness in bringing about improvement in teaching.

The criticism of external courses, together with a groundswell of professional opinion and practice, has encouraged more and more school-focused and school-based in-service activity. The TVEI-Related In-Service Training (TRIST) structures gave financial backing to such training events and the advent of the "Baker" day or school's professional development day has given added impetus.

Michael Fullan describes some positive findings on in-service training:

8   when complex teacher behaviours are the focus, school based programmes are more effective than university based programmes;

9   programmes based on demonstrations, supervised trials and feedback are more likely to accomplish their goals than are programmes which are based on theory and/or teachers are expected to store up ideas and practices for future use;

10   teachers contend that they learn best from other teachers concerning job related skills and practices, but also contend that they need some outside help from consultants who are capable of providing activities as in 9;

11   programmes in which teachers interact (share and provide assistance to each other) are more likely to accomplish their objectives;

12   programmes which provide different training experience for different teachers (i.e. are individualised) are more likely to accomplish their objectives;

13   programmes in which teachers participate as planners and decision-makers regarding in-service activities are more likely to have greater success;

14   teachers are more likely to benefit from in-service activities which are programme or project focused in which staff development is part and parcel of an overall plan to bring about improvement.

(Fullan in Hopkins (ed) 1986)

Bruce Joyce and Beverley Showers (1988) have researched the effectiveness of a number of components in training courses. These components are:

- presentation of theory or description of skill or strategy;

- modelling or demonstration of skills or models of teaching;

- practice in simulated classroom settings;

- structured and open-ended feedback (provision of information about performance);

- coaching for application (hands-on, in-classroom assistance with the transfer of skills and strategies to the classroom).

Their matrix, Diagram 2, graphically illustrates the effect of each type of training component on classroom practice.

Whilst theory or a lecture raises teachers' and librarians' awareness of the skills, they need to have them demonstrated, then to practice the new skills in safe, simulated settings, be given feedback, practice again and then to transfer and apply their new skills to their classroom (with help from peers and trainers) and then to integrate them into their teaching repertoire.

When each training component is used in concert it has a much greater power than when it is used alone.

The research of Joyce and Showers shows that the best knowledge we have to date suggests we use:

– integrated theory-demonstration-practice-feedback training pro-grammes to ensure skill development;

– considerable amounts of practice in simulated conditions to ensure we have control of the new skills;

– regular on-site coaching to facilitate vertical transfer – the develop-ment of new learning in the process of transfer;

– and prepare teachers to provide one another with the required coaching.

Diagram 2

Level of Impact

In-Service Training Component	Awareness	Knowledge	Skills	Application in classroom/ school
Presentation/ Theory	*			
Demonstration	*	*		
Practice in Simulated Settings	*	*	*	
Feedback on Performance	*	*	*	*
Coaching/ Assistance in the Classroom	*	*	*	*

Adapted from Joyce and Showers (1988)

Summary

In this section we have looked at the implementation of GCSE at a general level. Unlike its predecessors, GCSE demands that all students across the ability range carry out coursework assignments. This increase in coursework has placed great pressure on teachers and librarians. The GCSE Assessment Objectives call for students to have highly developed information skills. These skills of "learning how to learn" have to be developed early in the student's school career, and built upon throughout. There is also a demand for more resources which will need to be accessed by GCSE pupils.

GCSE calls for a radical rethink of teaching and learning styles, although for many teachers and schools GCSE builds upon the good practice they were carrying out before its inception. Teachers need help in building up their repertoire of teaching strategies. In particular they need support in such aspects of teaching as encouraging experiential learning and the teacher's role as facilitator. Therefore, teachers and librarians need ongoing in-service support in order further to develop their expertise. We examined current research findings on effective in-service education and training to see which type of training would best support teachers and librarians in their work. If they are to apply their new skills to the classroom they need in-service strategies which have a range of training components and which provide support at the classroom level.

3 Establishing a Whole-school Policy or Approach

In this section we look at information skills at the school level, with particular emphasis on GCSE. Taking account of implementation theory we look at how individuals and schools have attempted to introduce information skills. We first explore how an individual can make a difference, then move to the efforts made by two institutions to instigate a whole-school approach to information skills. We then turn to how other initiatives, such as school development planning and LMS, can be used to help in the development of information skills.

Although individuals can make a start on information skills work it is difficult to disseminate across departments and management structures. We found one chartered librarian working in a school with a dual-purpose library (i.e. it was used both as a public library and a school library) who contributed to information skills teaching in a small number of departments. She worked alongside the teacher, devising worksheets and teaching research skills. She was keen to foster the idea of progression and to encourage children to enjoy reading and research. She therefore instigated working in partnership with one local primary school. This involved her working alongside primary teachers and with their pupils both in the primary school and in the secondary library. The primary head noted that her contribution had made his pupils more aware of the need to plan and research for their projects and that their presentation skills had been enhanced. Her work has become a stepping-stone for more development in this area.

We discussed earlier the advantages of schools moving towards a whole-school approach to information skills. We have also argued that schools need to look at three stages in implementing such an innovation:

Initiation	Implementation	Institutionalisation
Stage	Stage	Stage

At the initiation stage the characteristic activities are:

- deciding to start
- launching the process
- deciding whether the school needs a whole-school approach to information skills
- commitment to the development.

The initiation of a whole-school approach to information skills is most likely to be successful if there is an active, strong advocate and a clear model (i.e. what does it mean, what would it look like in practice?). The following examples are from two of our case-study schools where they had been working towards a whole-school approach to information skills.

Rose School

In this school the active advocates were the school librarian and year head who had been on one of our two-day information skills courses. We have found this strategy of inviting the librarian plus another member of the teaching staff (preferably from the senior management team) a powerful method of in-service education and training. The two colleagues are able to give each other continuing support back at the school level. It helps to foster partnership between the librarian and teacher, it helps them keep the momentum going, and decreases the isolation felt by school librarians.

In order further to disseminate the idea of information skills, on their return to school, the two staff wrote a report for the whole staff outlining what they had learnt from the course and its implications and ways forward for their school. They saw their school's main needs as:

- support for teachers in developing information skills;

- open access to the library;

- coordination of work to allow for reinforcement and prevent unnecessary replication.

In order to begin more systematic work on information skills they decided to review what was already being done by their colleagues. Thus later the following term, they followed up with a questionnaire to ascertain the information skills teaching and needs in each subject area. A covering letter by the year head was sent with the questionnaire outlining the need for change and the proposals. Teachers were therefore clear about the aims of the questionnaire. There were rewards implicit in the advocates' proposals for development of information skills in the whole curriculum, e.g. benefits to pupils, and the resources centre offer to construct suitable materials to support teachers. The librarian felt the role of the year head was crucial in getting teachers' support:

It was important that the questionnaire went out from a

teacher, it has a lot more clout if it comes from a teacher with practical teaching experience in a classroom.

(School librarian)

Once the questionnaire returns were analysed a summary was sent to the whole staff so that they were all kept informed of what was going on. This is another crucial strategy – to keep all of the staff informed and not to keep the innovation to a small group, as this only builds up a mystique. This could either lead to resentment on the part of the rest of the staff or, equally damaging to the innovation, to teachers feeling that the matter is being dealt with by others – the "experts". As we said earlier, information skills teaching is the concern of *every* teacher regardless of subject.

The librarian then spoke to each department to ask *how* they are teaching information skills and whether they have examples of interesting practice which they are willing to share. She now has a clearer view of who is doing what and how, and is also building up a resource bank of examples of interesting practice to share with new members of staff or other subject areas.

Their questionnaire/survey of information skills provision has proved a useful base to begin working towards a whole-school approach. Gaps in provision have been identified and plans are under way to deal with this. For example one department highlighted their need for pupils to have notemaking and spider diagram skills. The survey found that other departments were indeed covering these, and thus the development team were able to put the various departments in touch with each other. However, the librarian offered further to develop such skills if staff wished. Another member of staff expressed a willingness to assist staff with teaching note-making skills. Those areas which seemed to need reinforcing between Year 7 and Year 10 were alphabetical skills, the use of the Dewey system and the use of external resources. The librarian, with support from various subject staff, plans to work on these areas for development in the future.

The whole process of reporting back from an in-service education and training session, leading school-based in-service education and training on study skills across the curriculum, looking at ways forward which might help their particular school, working closely with a number of individual teachers and subjects and offering practical help has raised the profile of the library in the school. The chartered librarian has had her hours of work increased under LMS from 10 to 25. There is thus more chance of pupils and staff having open access to the library. Whilst there is always room for more resourcing this is a significant move forward. The whole process of debate and discussion has drawn in a wide range of staff, another important factor in the successful implementation of an innovation.

Their future plans include a working party or study skills committee with members drawn from each of the subject areas. To assist Year 10 students they are discussing the possibility of a pre-GCSE refresher course, and also some kind of support structure, possibly library based, for Year 10 and Year 11. In order to build a sound foundation upon which GCSE work will be based they are planning a cross-curricular programme of skills development for all Year 7 pupils.

Violet School

We found a similar strategy working in Violet School. Here the chartered librarian was full-time, had clerical support and made a significant contribution to information skills teaching. She was already working closely with a number of departments in planning students' work and teaching alongside her colleagues. There was an active library committee with clear support from the senior management team. Despite the high profile of the library in the school there were a number of departments which did not seem to use the available resources. The advent of GCSE increased the number of students coming to do individual research. There was an active, committed library committee with representatives from each subject area, a member of the senior management team and the professional librarian. This is vital when schools are attempting to integrate information/ learning skills across the curriculum. Support is required both from the senior management team and subject areas. The library committee felt that the school was ready to move towards a whole-school approach to information skills. Although there were pockets of exemplary practice in information skills teaching in the school, they were not systematically linked to one another:

> There's nothing going on cross-curricular in school in a structured way. The problem is it's got to be structured. The Year 7 did study skills as part of their library session but it was decontextualised, four years on they had forgotten. The skills hadn't been referred to or built on in the rest of the curriculum. They need to be regularly used and taught.

> People in school see knowledge as a commodity you can pass around, not as something we've all got to build on.
> (Head of year)

Nevertheless, many staff were aware of the need for these skills and the importance of them being taught within subject areas. In the past subject departments had drawn up skills lists which were circulated to other departments for information. They had already had some in-service support, as the previous year one staff professional development day was led by Sharon Markless, and the topic was information skills. The library committee had drawn up and circulated a recently drawn-up library policy which highlighted the role of the library and librarian in the curriculum, and they had asked for any comments or additions.

In order to find out exactly where the school was in terms of its information skills provision, the library committee drew up an information skills questionnaire to ascertain which subject departments were covering particular aspects.

Individual members of the library committee took the questionnaire to their subject department meetings to explain the purpose of the survey. The librarian was responsible for collection and analysis of the data together with any follow-up visits to departments.

At the same time, the school was developing its liaison work with primary feeder schools and investigating the skills taught.

> The primary school views are useful because they have a cross-curricular view. The primary schools have done this work but it hasn't been built on so there is no transfer.
>
> (Teacher i/c liaison)

This primary liaison work was given time and financial backing. A member of staff began to look at the feeder primary schools with a view to drawing up a skills profile. A draft list was drawn up and circulated to each department for comment. A working party was set up consisting of members of the secondary school's staff and those from the primary schools. They developed a transfer document which gave an indication of each pupil's reading and mathematics attainment, and how pupils worked as individuals and as part of a group. Finally they asked for a project which the pupil had been working on in the primary school which could be developed during the first few weeks at the secondary school. In addition, several members of the secondary staff visit the primary schools to work with pupils, and the primary heads visit the secondary school department meetings with examples of their primary children's work. The librarian also visits the primary schools to facilitate closer links. These strategies help the subject staff and the school librarian by giving a clearer indication of the skills already possessed by the new entrants.

We don't want to be constantly reinventing the wheel, we want to build on the work they've already done in the primary schools.

(Teacher i/c liaison)

It gives them something to build on, helping to prevent oversight of important aspects of information skills and to avoid the unnecessary duplication of work. The National Curriculum has given added impetus to this liaison work. The school is planning to integrate information skills into each subject's syllabus. This is an important stage and staff will need to keep the momentum going.

Summary

Both schools outlined here are in the early stages of implementing a whole-school approach. Unlike the first example of a librarian working at an individual level they had support from other members of staff, including the senior management. There had been in-service support either for themselves or for members of their staff. If we refer back to the need to take note of the change process we know that at the implementation stage in any development the characteristic activities are:

*   goal setting

*   designing action plans

*   carrying out these plans.

Both schools had set goals and made plans for future action and for the next stages of development.

These two examples were not the only ones we found of schools attempting to establish a whole-school approach to information skills but they are indicative of the type of activity we found. They share some common features:

−   active, enthusiastic advocates;

−   involvement of a member or members of the senior management team;

−   involvement of a professional school librarian, with high status in the school;

- appreciation of the fact that these skills need to be built on from an early age and constantly reinforced;

- conducting a review of what the school was already doing on the information skills front;

- involvement of as many staff as possible in the innovation;

- in-service support for both teaching staff and the school librarian;

- resources, in the form of either time or money;

- teachers could see the benefits of the innovation to their teaching;

- encouragement of collaborative working;

- sharing expertise and networking between departments/library;

- they were working with each other, starting from where teachers were, not trying to impose a "package".

Nevertheless, schools are finding it difficult to implement whole-school approaches to information skills teaching. Such a change is complex and cannot be achieved overnight. Energy is needed at each stage of the development, not just at the beginning, if the innovation is to be integrated into the curriculum of the school.

There are other strategies which might be used to give impetus for this work such as school development planning.

School Development Plans

In order for whole-school approaches to be successful one of our advisory questionnaire respondents believes that the head is the key to success:

> The desirability of such a move has been around, registered and supported for 15 years or more. What we have found is that such a move requires so radical a redistribution of already inadequate funds, so momentous a change in, and extension of, teacher training, so demanding a reorientation of learning opportunities provided, so complete a dismantling of current curriculum/timetable organisation, that only those rare places where leadership at head level

identifies this issue as the single top priority can thorough-going progress toward this goal be achieved.

(LEA Chief Adviser)

Certainly the literature on educational change reinforces this view that clear leadership is vital to the success of an innovation. In our two previous examples of schools attempting to have a whole-school approach to information skills there was clear senior management support, and this is needed to sustain the innovation.

Given the number of seemingly conflicting initiatives with which heads have had to grapple it is not surprising that many are reluctant to give time and energy to information skills.

However, schools now have to identify their needs each year through the School Development Plan. Thus staff, including the librarian may highlight information skills or teaching/learning strategies as an area for the head and governors to consider for further development.

Development planning encourages the school to look at:

– where the school is now;

– what changes it needs to make;

– how it can manage those changes over time;

– recognise whether their management of the change has been successful.

The plan will bring together national and LEA policies and initiatives and the school's aims, values, existing achievements and its future development needs. There are four processes involved in development planning:

* audit – the school reviews its strengths and weaknesses;

* constructing the plan – the school selects priorities for development and turns them into specific targets;

* implementation – of the planned priorities and targets;

* evaluation – is the implementation successful?

One of the common threads which runs through many of the recent initiatives in schools is the need for changes in teaching and learning style. If the school chooses to look at teaching and learning styles as a priority, each member of staff including the librarian can take part in collecting data for the audit. If this is selected as a priority area for further development, and this is usually the prerogative of senior management and governors, then the school needs to develop detailed action plans with specific targets for the following year. This would be the teachers' working document and includes tasks, responsibilities and success criteria.

The development plan embraces and shapes all aspects of school planning. For example if teaching and learning styles are chosen as a priority area, then appropriate in-service education and training and resources may have to be set aside to back up the development. There may need to be changes in the school's organisation, e.g. from an eight-period to four-period day to facilitate more student-centred styles of learning. Thus it is a systematic process.

In the same way LMS could help schools which wish to move towards a more integrated approach to information or learning skills teaching. Schools can now choose how to spend their resources, and if developing a central library to support student learning is a priority then they can spend money in that way.

School development planning gives individuals the opportunity to feed needs to the senior management and for priorities to be selected. LMS gives schools the ability to develop and resource their most important needs. At the time of our research these two initiatives were in their infancy but were mentioned as possible ways forward by the schools and LEAs we visited.

In the following section we look at examples of school-based in-service training activities in schools where there has been clear leadership from the head and senior management team.

4 School-based In-service Education and Training Support

In this section we turn to examples of school-based in-service support. These are taken from our case-study schools and their respective LEA or support mechanism.

We have highlighted in an earlier section the need for clarity about the innovation, and for teachers and librarians to have a clear model and their need for ongoing in-service support. At first this support may take the form of highlighting the new skills which they may have to master and to help alleviate the inevitable anxiety they face as they come to terms with the innovation. Subsequently "top-up" training may be required as they tentatively try out new techniques and want feedback on their performance.

All schools had received some form of in-service education and training when GCSE was introduced through the "cascade" system referred to earlier. Gradually LEAs and schools themselves began to take over responsibility for training. School-based in-service education and training allows for the individual needs of a school to be met and can be directly related to the classroom of the participating teachers. We argued earlier that teachers and librarians need in-service education and training which has a range of training components. These are theory, demonstration, practice and feedback.

Primrose School

The newly created Resource Based Learning Centre (RBLC) is managed by a senior teacher, Joanne Jones, with a full-time librarian/ technician paid for by TVEI. There is, therefore, access to the centre all day. Students and teachers "can work shoulder to shoulder". The RBLC houses a selection of book stock and project packs with tables and chairs or an easy-chair section. There is an adjoining computer area for individual student use, plus a studio where students can use video or audio tape-recording equipment for their project work. During the field visit students were using the word processors to edit and produce an assignment, whilst others were in the studio recording poems they had written. Individuals from a range of subject areas were conducting their individual research amongst the book and pamphlet stock.

Information Skills. In Year 7, during English lessons, students are taught over a six-week period how to use the RBLC. The outcome of this work is a project. However, Joanne is attempting to encourage *every* member of staff to become a study skills tutor, to spread information skills across the curriculum. Strategies she has used to help students with their assignments are:

–   posters showing the Dewey classification system in each classroom;

–   designing an assignment form which is filled in by the student and signed by the teacher before the student goes to the RBLC. This form indicates the research topic and possible information sources.

The aim of the assignment form was to encourage students to formulate research questions and to plan their research before going to the RBLC. However, some staff were not clear about the purposes of the form, so Joanne worked with them at an individual and departmental level to explain the rationale. She sees open communication and involving staff in the developments as vital for moving forward. There is a working party set up to decide the role and function of the RBLC and this reports back to every subject area. Joanne continually gives teachers in-classroom support for students' GCSE or other assignment work.

In-service Education and Training Day. However, it was decided to move further towards a more coherent approach to information skills teaching, and so a professional development day was set aside for information skills development. Joanne approached each head of department and asked them first to discuss with their department members, then to draw up a plan of work which would lend itself to supported self study (see Diagrams 3 and 4). The time that they expended on this planning exercise would be repaid in departmental time to be given during the in-service education and training day. Each department was asked to check the resources available in the RBLC before setting the task which another group of teachers was going to undertake. Joanne paired the departments, e.g. Music with Drama. The Drama department would set the task for the Music team and vice versa.

Diagram 3

To Head of............... Department

As outlined at Heads of Department meeting:

I would like to take some time* (departmental or elsewhere) in preparing a topic from your syllabus or National Curriculum targets which a group of colleagues could research and present. They may work as a group or in pairs.

They will have about half an hour to receive instructions and record guidelines for the work. One hour on the actual research – half an hour presentation followed by discussion.

Because of the artificial timescale the topic must perforce be simple and may well take the form of a question, e.g. How many types of...? Uses for...? What conditions...? What contributions...? etc., etc.

Consider the group's likely familiarity or interest in the subject. What are *our* resources? What skills of enquiry have you built into the topic? How will you assess the outcome? Will you build in peer group assessment? What statements of outcome will you make? Could they be in the form of Record of Achievement targets?

When you have prepared your plan could I have a copy *before* the event together with additional details on the attached form.

* You will be amply recompensed for the time spent on the above, as time will be given for departmental work on the INSET day.

Diagram 4

INSET

INFORMATION RETRIEVAL AND THE USE OF RBLC TRAINING

(Information Skills and the National Curriculum)

Please remember that preparation work is part of the training. Complete and return to Mrs Jones as soon as possible.

What information is needed? What is the recipient(s) being asked to find out?

What sources of information are there?

How would you like it recording and presenting?

What "audience" have you in mind?

At the beginning of the in-service education and training day Joanne spoke to the whole staff for 10 minutes to outline the rationale for the day. Departments went into their pairs, the one setting the first task gave a 30-minute briefing to the "research" group. The researchers filled in an activity record (see Diagram 5) which outlined what they planned to do.

Diagram 5

ACTIVITY RECORD (Information retrieval)

Complete at briefing:

NAME...........................DEPARTMENT......................

1. Description of Task Set:

2. Learning Style (Individual/Paired/Group etc)

3. Resources required (If they have been found please tick)

4. Outcome: form of presentation
   e.g. written, visual, drama, role, talk, recording... other

5. What is to be assessed
   e.g. perseverance, creativity, ingenuity, enterprise, teamwork

6. How will it be assessed?
   e.g. self, peer, teacher.

The "researchers" had 70 minutes to do their task, whilst the others had their departmental meeting (the pay-back for the departmental planning time spent previous to the in-service education and training day).

Presentation – the "researchers" had 30 minutes to give their presentation and to evaluate the session (see Diagram 6).

Diagram 6

EVALUATION SHEET

RESOURCE BASED LEARNING CENTRE – ACTIVITY DAY

1. INDIVIDUAL LEARNING – Pupil's point of view
   What have you found that a pupil might have found helpful/encouraging/useful if he/she were pursuing individual study?

2. What have you found that a pupil might discover was unhelpful/lacking etc?

1. INDIVIDUAL LEARNING – Teacher's point of view
   As another strategy for learning what do you find the RBLC has to offer?

2. What does it lack?

Then the roles were reversed.

Summary

Comments from staff on the day were positive. They had a deeper understanding of the problems faced by their students when conducting assignments. They were also more aware of the value of the RBLC, and had a clearer knowledge of what it had to offer, as well as what it lacked. Since the in-service education and training day (less than two weeks before the field visit) five more members of staff had asked how to book the RBLC.

Lessons learned from the in-service education and training included:

– assignments need to be carefully planned and have to be achievable in the set time;

- resources need to be available to meet the assignment needs;

- a wide range and type of resources are necessary – video cameras, video tapes, project packs, newspaper cuttings, journals, photographic facilities, drawing board, and equipment to aid presentation and so forth;

- full-time staff on duty to help students with individual assignments;

- how to work in groups;

- provision has to be made for a variety of presentations and not just written ones;

- people like to share their hard work with others and display/ present their work for all to see.

The in-service education and training had been planned so that teachers had to go through the same process as students doing GCSE or other assignments. In this way teachers were able to meet and overcome the same problems faced by their students. This was a strategy used by several of the librarians in our case-study schools. When leading in-service education and training sessions for their school staff they give teachers difficult tasks to carry out in the library, yet such tasks are ones that some teachers expected of pupils. The tasks set are either unrealistic, too wide-ranging, or there are no resources available to meet the task. This encourages staff to be aware of the problems students face and to liaise more closely with the librarian before setting such tasks for pupils. They are now able to encourage the pupils themselves to formulate research questions before heading off to the library. It also encourages closer work between the librarian and subject teachers. Joanne was able to follow up by supporting the classroom teacher at the individual or departmental level.

Plantation LEA

In another LEA, we visited the advisory teacher for resource-based learning; she had been active in running in-service sessions for schools and in schools. She had drawn up a resource package on staff development for teaching and learning which is being piloted by several schools in the LEA. One activity, on integrating learning skills into syllabus planning, could be used for training sessions with heads of department or faculty.

Activity 1 Aims to:

- *raise heads of departments' awareness of students' learning skills needs;*
- *highlight where these skills are taught;*
- *coordinate the school's work on these skills;*
- *develop learning strategies in their subject area.*

The heads of departments were given a brief introduction to learning skills and individually read Terry Brake's Tools for Learning *and filled the pro forma based on his framework of skills. An example of the first part of the pro forma is shown in Diagram 7.*

Diagram 7

Skills course	*Tick*	*Subject area or separate*
1. *Thinking Forward* Brainstorm *Create topic web* *Sequence activities* *(flow charts)* *Plan time* *Identify key words* *(precursor to note making)*		

Their task was to identify and tick any skills teaching which might require specific teaching or reinforcement and then note where in the curriculum they would expect them to be taught. In groups they looked at skills needs of a particular year group of students and agreed lists of skills and subject context for the learning skills to be taught. They made a poster/flip chart to display these skills and needs to the other year group working groups. The next stage was to investigate ways of publicising their findings. Some schools have put up posters round the staffroom to show skills needs and subject areas' contributions.

This in-service strategy raised heads of departments' awareness of pupils' learning skills needs and where they could be acquired in the curriculum. It allowed for all other members of staff to share in the findings of the working groups. It began to move the school toward a coordinated strategy for learning skills and encouraged staff to build on or develop the skills identified. The group activities and the poster displays raised subject teachers' awareness of what are the needs and skills of other subject areas.

Another strategy used by a number of schools for raising whole-staff awareness and to agree priorities for development was a card-sort exercise.

Activity 2

The leader of the training activity gives out 16 statements.

Example of statements:
(individual schools can devise those most appropriate to themselves)

> *Commitment of subject teachers to using and reinforcing information skills*

> *Open access to library for teachers and students*

> *Senior management team to give priority and lead*

> *INSET to support staff...*

These statements are cut out individually. Each person then chooses nine which they think are most important when a school wants to develop a whole-school approach to information skills. Each person then puts their nine statements in order:

$$
\begin{array}{ccc}
 & 1 & \\
2 & & 2 \\
3 & 3 & 3 \\
4 & & 4 \\
 & 5 &
\end{array}
$$

Then into pairs to try to reach agreement on the nine most important, and in what order. Into fours to reach agreement on the nine and in what order, discussing reasons for selection and rejection. A spokesperson reports back to the plenary session on their group of four's priorities.

This activity raises a whole range of issues which can be discussed and developed further. It provides a basis for future development and establishes priorities for action. It also serves to enable all teachers and the librarian in the school to share a common vocabulary.

Activity 3

Another typical in-service strategy we found was one similar to that outlined by Michael Marland (1981) "Helping Pupils Learn How to Find Out". This activity was designed by Dai Hounsell (see Hounsell and Martin (1983) for other hints and tips on running courses).

Teachers are asked to think of a recent assignment they have given a class and jot down notes about it using this type of framework:

> *Class/form:*
> *Assignment topic:*
> *Title or questions set:*
> *Time allowed:*
> *Format: (e.g. essay, map etc.)*
> *Help given: (e.g. film during lesson)*

On completion the leader of the training session then gives out the nine question steps.

> **What do I need to do?**
> *(formulate and analyse need)*
>
> **Where could I go?**
> *(identify and appraise likely sources)*
>
> **How do I get to the information?**
> *(trace and locate individual resources)*
>
> **Which resources shall I use?**
> *(examine, select and reject individual resources)*
>
> **How shall I use the resources?**
> *(interrogate resources)*
>
> **What should I make a record of?**
> *(record and store information)*
>
> **Have I got the information I need?**
> *(interpret, analyse, synthesise, evaluate)*

61

How should I present it?
(present, communicate)

What have I achieved?
(evaluate)

(Marland (ed) 1981)

The teachers then have to answer the questions in the light of the assignment they set. In pairs they discuss their assignments and ask each other clarifying questions.

The pairs then form fours but this time each partner acts as spokesperson for the other describing their assignments to the other two people. Once everyone is familiar with all four assignments they then select one for further study. Using that one assignment as an example they then draw up a poster (see Diagram 8) showing skills they assume students already have and skills they expect to develop in the course of the assignment. The final column shows the skills that they expect to assess:

Diagram 8

POSTER

Class: *Topic:*   *Time:*

Question(s)

Help given

Skills assumed   *Skills to be acquired*

Skills to be assessed

The posters are displayed and then the whole group look at the issues raised and the implications for future assignment work.

In one school the staff developed this work by drawing up a set of guidelines for students in GCSE assignments. They tried to encourage staff to be more consistent over issues like the layout of projects, e.g. an index, bibliography and references section.

The advisory teacher in collaboration with other teachers in the LEA had produced a range of materials for in-service courses. Schools could take packages "off the shelf" or adapt them to their own needs.

Summary

These examples indicate some of the work that we saw in schools and LEAs. The whole staff is encouraged to think through the issues connected with information skills and to plan ways forward. By involving the whole staff a common understanding of the innovation is developed and a support network can be built up. In addition there is more chance of disseminating the good practice which already exists in some classrooms or departments.

There are of course many more examples of school-based in-service work. The in-service training carried out for TVEI and TVEI Extension has developed teaching/learning styles and currently the needs of the National Curriculum are being met by extensive in-service training. Similarly, teacher appraisal will help teachers to develop teaching strategies. The classroom observation phase allows the observer (usually the appraiser) to give the appraisee positive feedback on performance. He or she can then work with the appraisee to support developments. Similarly, the observer can pick up ideas and different strategies to take back to his or her own teaching situation.

5 The Classroom Level – Learning Strategies

We have looked at the schools' and teachers' development in information or learning skills and we now turn to the students in the classroom. It is the learning experience of the students which is our ultimate focus as educators. Just as we need to start from where schools and teachers are, so too we need to start from where the students are in their development. We are concerned with helping students learn how to learn, for the only person who is educated is the one who has learned how to adapt and change. We are living in a time of rapid change so students need to learn flexibility and adaptability.

In the words of Carl Rogers, "no knowledge is secure, ... only the process of seeking knowledge gives a basis for security. Changingness, a reliance on PROCESS rather than upon static knowledge, is the only thing that makes any real sense as a goal for education in the modern world" (Rogers 1969). An understanding of the strategies for learning and self-knowledge enables students to control the process of learning and be responsible for it. We need to value the learning styles the students have and build on them, and to encourage flexibility. Teachers therefore need to employ a range of teaching strategies and to build up students' information skills or abilities to learn how to learn.

The following examples are strategies used by some of our case-study schools at the classroom or library level. In the first example, Foxglove, we see how the Humanities department has structured information and library skills into its first-year work with students (Year 7).

Foxglove School

In this school there is a chartered librarian working with a number of departments. During our field visits we observed Year 7 Humanities lessons in the library. Information skills are built into the syllabus as are the resources which could be used. Students begin Humanities with a general overview of the skills involved in the subject followed by library skills or atlas skills. The syllabus lists the skills used in the atlas sessions as:

> Information finding skills
> Appreciation of differences in maps
> Ability to use contents, index, etc.
> Ability to extract simple information

Ability to answer simple questions
Social skills centred at individual and group level.

By week two or three students are involved in library skills:

KEY IDEAS. Library Skills: the library is a major resource centre for information, ideas, data, etc. relating to Humanities. It is vital that the pupils know how to use the library resources to the maximum effect.

PUPIL/TEACHER ACTIVITIES/CONTENT. This library activity follows on from the introduction. It is to be carried out in the week following or the week after depending on library bookings.

Lesson 1. Introduction to the library, its layout/classification, etc. with particular reference to Humanities. Session led by librarian. After an introduction pupils to begin set tasks.

Lesson 2. Given over to word linkage search.

Lesson 3. Spider diagrams and completion for homework. See pupil sheets for set tasks. The idea is to find the word in the middle (e.g. motte; bailey; knight; rampart). Sheets are at three levels. You may like to start everyone at level 1 – those who move through quickly may go on to level 2 or even level 3, missing out level 2. (Answer sheet supplied.)

Everyone should complete at least level 1. The next exercise is based on word association. Pupils can be allocated a word (e.g. earthquake) – see pupil sheet and complete spider diagram. Three chosen words from the spider diagram are to be expanded into paragraphs. Complete for homework.

There is differentiation by task and by outcome.

SKILLS USED/TESTED. Information finding. Study skills:
Extracting information
Communication – putting over ideas in a) diagrams
                                        b) written forms
Ability to summarise – spider diagrams. Practical – use of reference materials.

N.B. The *content* is the vehicle for the *skill*.
                        (extracts from Humanities syllabus)

By week 3 pupils are looking at: what is history? How do historians study the past? Historians do not all reach the same conclusions. Pupils use a wide range of resources for this part of the syllabus and the skills used include investigative skills, use of evidence, making deductions, asking historical questions, recognising evidence as opposed to opinion, recognising simple bias, and observational skills.

Week 4 is use of grid references.

One of our field visits coincided with week 5 "History Time". In the lesson observed, students were in the library researching a group of pictures from history. The pictures were from all periods of historical time and students had to use their skill to date them. They had previously worked on timelines and on historical language and concepts, e.g. AD, BC, century. They had drawn up a timeline for their family.

The picture search exercise we observed was "a practical attempt to look at skills in chronology/time sequence and to build on detective skills – evidence." They were given some pictures to date, and an activity sheet which asked the students to look carefully at the seven pieces of picture evidence, to name the picture, describe what they see and what clues are available to date the picture. They were using a number of books, textbooks, library books from many sections of the library. They worked in mixed groups of four and clearly enjoyed their task. Their ability to analyse the pictures was admirable.

> It must be from early this century because it's a photograph.

> They're wearing those baggy trousers like Tudors wear.

> I think that was more than 100 years ago because we don't have gas lamps any more.

> I saw something like that in a museum. It's from Sutton Hoo.

> If we look at a book about houses we might find one that looks like this one.

> My grandad wore something like that.

Summary

Information skills were built into the syllabus with clear guidance for both teachers and students. There were clear indications given of when

66

and how students could work as groups or individuals. There were also lists of resource requirements and other resources which could be used. The skills to be assessed were also noted. The librarian worked alongside the teachers and students.

Primrose School

In this example we see the librarian's attempt to help students with their research for GCSE or other assignments.

Students have in their form rooms a copy of the Dewey classification index to encourage familiarity with the RBLC system. The senior teacher in charge of the RBLC, Joanne Jones, works alongside subject teachers helping students with research skills for their GCSE, or other, assignments. She is currently piloting a form for students to use before and during their visit to the RBLC (see Diagram 9). This form is designed to try to help students formulate research questions before coming to the RBLC and therefore to use the RBLC more efficiently.

Students' early attempts to use this form have been varied, from those who state that they want to know about "churches" to the more focused "various mythical or real costumes". Resources required drew the same range of responses from "books" to a much wider perception of "books, pictures, film? slides?".

Students' planning skills for time use were also varied, from one student who thought he would take "whatever" time (in fact only 10 minutes) to find out about churches to another who specified one hour to research the mythical or real costumes.

Diagram 9

PRO FORMA FOR RBLC USE

TO BE *COMPLETED BY PUPIL* AND HANDED TO
LIBRARIAN/STAFF ON DUTY

NAME _____ FORM _____ DATE _____

SUBJECT _____ TEACHER _____

1. *I am using the Resource Based Learning Centre because
this is what I want to know:

2. These are the resources I need:

3. Library headings I will try:

Ask staff on duty to suggest further Dewey numbers etc. here if
you wish:

4. Amount of time I expect to spend on this: _____

5. Where will this work take place?

Signed _____ Agreed and countersigned by _____
    pupil's signature   teacher's signature

*Please ensure that the pupil knows exactly what s/he wants to
find rather than a "a topic on", "research", "a book on...."

List of books and items removed from the RBLC:

The initial pro forma has been adapted in the light of experience to
include Dewey numbers against the resources to be used, a return time
to the classroom, and a statement on the form that "browsing for ideas
is an acceptable alternative".

To encourage students to evaluate their research process, Joanne has
designed an assignment review on the reverse side of the pro forma.
Although this was not yet widely used by the students and teachers
at the time of the field visit (spring 1990), it was intended to be

implemented and included in students' Records of Achievement files. The pro forma, together with Joanne's individual work with students, gives them a structure for their research. As outlined in the previous chapter, the staff at Primrose had taken part in an in-service training session which had familiarised them with this way of working.

Violet School

The library is extensively used by both whole classes and those doing individual research (see Appendix 2 for analysis of library use). The chartered librarian, Catherine Adams, is involved in library induction courses working alongside members of the Science department. She also works with individual teachers and students. In this outline we look at the work of the Geography and Science departments and their attempt to integrate information skills.

The Geography department GCSE course follows the LEAG B (London and East Anglian Group) Examination Board syllabus where there is a substantial coursework component. Violet students undertake three coursework assignments involving data collection:

1. Fieldwork – this involves a coastal study. There is more teacher direction in this first coursework assignment as students have not been familiarised with the information skills required of them at an earlier stage in the school.

2. Based on secondary sources – students use the library where they access Prestel, and use books and project packs. A typical example of such coursework would be "Acid Rain".

3. In this final assignment teachers encourage students to plan their work in more detail themselves. The assignment is usually locally based, for example, "Should Violet Road be pedestrianised?" or "There is a parking problem in the town, how can we solve it?"

The department gives students guidance on presenting coursework and collecting data (see Appendix 3). It has produced a guidance sheet showing the Examination Board's critique of students' coursework, which enables Violet School students to avoid certain failings and gives hints and tips on how to produce satisfactory work. This advice is based on that given by LEAG in its document "Underway with GCSE Geography" (LEAG 1987). Finally it issues students with the marking scheme which is also outlined in the LEAG guidelines. The department is keen to help students tackle research problems such as:

notemaking skills, everyone assumes that children miraculously know how it's done.

(Head of department)

The department is working on building up these skills lower down the school than Year 10, but it will be some time before all students have a sound knowledge base to work on.

Similarly the Science department is working on making information skills more explicit for all its students. In Year 7 students have sessions in the library with their Science teacher and the librarian to learn how to use the library. In the main, Catherine Adams uses worksheets from the Carel Press which are relevant to this work. As the department has become more familiar with these it has designed its own sheets to meet the particular needs of the subject and students. The Science department uses the Warwick Science scheme. In Year 7 students have to study classification so the Science teacher takes the group to the library for two sessions where students learn about the Dewey classification scheme. The following lesson they are in the laboratory where they classify their class in terms of eye and hair colour and so forth. Thus work in the library is reinforced during the subject and throughout the syllabus.

Year 7 Science students take part in a role play exercise "Murder at Cold Farm". They are teams of forensic scientists investigating a murder. To set the scene they watch a videotape of Crimebusters to see how the police would tackle such a problem. Working with the Drama department they do a role play on murder in the Drama studio. During the course of our fieldwork we observed the group in the laboratory where they worked in teams of four forensic scientists trying to sift through the clues and find the murderer. The clues were a footprint, typewriter writing, a pen, fibres and soil found at the scene of the crime. Their task was to find out who did it and why. The students worked well as a group and worked logically through the evidence. They presented their findings to the rest of the group. There were clear worksheets on how to set about the task, what to do and how to present it.

By Year 10 notemaking and project skills are reinforced for the GCSE assignment work. In one of the Year 10 lessons observed in the library, students were beginning their research on one of three topics to do with Food, Diet and Additives. The previous lesson had been spent working on notemaking skills. Some students were working collaboratively to design a questionnaire to ascertain whether Year 7 students ate a balanced diet. Others were trying to find out what a balanced diet was, whilst one girl was using project packs, books and Communitel to find out why additives are used in food.

We observed two Chemistry lessons where a mixed ability class of Year 10 students were beginning a GCSE assignment. The teacher outlined the assignment stating it had to be Chemistry based, and the time span was four one-hour lessons plus four weeks of homework. He underlined the need to plan it, state the purpose of the study and to bear in mind the time available. Students were told the marking scheme. During the first lesson they were to plan the assignment using a worksheet outlining the question steps. Diagram 10 is page one of the project planner.

The pages which followed were questions to do with the other question steps (see Marland (ed) 1981).

Most of the students we spoke to found it helpful to plan in this way. The teacher allowed the students to get on with their assignment but was there if they needed help. He continued to monitor their progress by asking such questions as: What topic are you doing? Is that possible in the timescale? What resources have you used or will you use?

In the following lesson observed, students had made progress. A number had written to organisations and had replies. One girl was investigating the use of animals in research and had telephoned and written to organisations. We asked if she was arguing in favour of animal experiments or what.

> I'm aiming to write a balanced piece of work, setting out the arguments on both sides. It's interesting [points to envelopes of information] one of these groups is for, this one's against and they give arguments for their side. This one realises that some experiments are necessary but doesn't really believe in it. I shall look at them all and try to give a balance, though of course I'm against it. But I don't want it to be biased.
>
> (Student)

Diagram 10

---

1. What do I have to do?

Name _____ Class _____ Date _____

What is the project for?

Subject _____ Exam _____

What is the topic? _____

How much time do you have? _____

What particular aspects are you interested in? _____

_____

Do you have time to cover them all? If not, make a selection of
the most interesting aspects _____

_____

What do you know about already? Give a brief outline _____

_____

Another student had a clear idea of where he was going:

> I'm doing an introduction because I think I need to say
> what the project will cover. I think it's important. Then I'm
> going to put headings and describe each additive. At the
> end I will say what I've learned and what each does.
> (Student)

Despite this, and other students' attempts to use a wide range of
information and draw balanced conclusions there were still one or two
students copying chunks of text with little idea of where they were
going.

Another student was being very enterprising. She had done an
assignment on nuclear power in Social Studies last term:

I had all the information; it was just a question of using different parts for different aspects. I thought, well I'd already got the info for the other assignment, so I might as well use it.

(Student)

Despite encouragement to present the assignments in any way they wished all of the students except one intended to submit a written piece of work. The exception was a boy considering submitting tape recordings.

Whilst the Chemistry group were working in the library there were others doing individual research for other subjects such as GCSE History and English.

We asked one of these boys how he set about his assignment:

I think the teacher helps us too much. There's too much guidance. I'd rather have a free hand. Some people in the class need a lot more help, but the rest of us can do it on our own.

(Student)

His neighbour chipped in:

They question us but don't give enough time to answer or go off and research. The teacher asks it in such a way we give his answer so all the projects end up the same.

(Student)

There is a fine line between guidance and too much teacher direction. The students themselves make the point that each one of them is different, with differing needs. Their anxiety to get to the library and research for themselves reflects the high profile of both the library and librarian in the school.

Poppy Sixth Form Centre

In this example we look at library induction, individual and class research in the library and issues for students in moving toward independent learning.

A large number of students are involved in GCSE, some are "re-take" whilst others are doing GCSEs to be completed in one year rather than the usual two years. In order to make overall planning easier for both students and teachers a member of staff has responsibility for coordinating GCSE. He has drawn up a year planner which consists of a list of dates for coursework completion, orals, practicals and written examinations, together with parents' evening dates. Staff are encouraged to set their coursework with due regard to other subjects' requirements whilst keeping to the general framework set by the Examination Boards. This matrix, given to all students and staff, is a useful personal organiser for both staff and students and helps to avoid some of the coursework overload commented upon in HMI reports (e.g. DES 1988b, 1988c).

The centre has a chartered librarian with clerical support. The library suite consists of a library, resources room and room for silent work. The students come from a wide range of feeder secondary, comprehensive or independent schools. Some had come from schools where independent research had been encouraged and promoted and where the library enjoyed a high profile. Not all students had this experience, and therefore the chartered librarian, Elaine, arranged library induction courses for every tutor group and for the subject departments. As one of the students commented:

> At the beginning of the year all my subject teachers showed the class how to use the library. This was good and as a result I have used the library for reference.

Others were not so fortunate:

> [Those] who appeared to have missed the induction, though this must have been difficult as a tutorial introduction as well as ones through subject areas had been arranged, found their way by trial and error. Not understanding the system led to one student's not using the library though he "might need it for reference later". One admitted to the embarrassment lack of knowledge might lead to: "I am still a little uncertain as to where each subject area is and feel a bit lost when trying to look for specific book topics. You feel stupid looking down each aisle trying to find your subject."
>
> (Vice principal)

The librarian had collections of each subject's syllabus, examination papers and reading lists. She had produced, in conjunction with subject teachers, library-use worksheets which were specific to the subject and concerned a particular coursework assignment. Students came to the library individually or with subject staff for whole lessons, often for the duration of a specific assignment. The more familiar the students became with the library, the more confident they were:

> I'm finding my way round the library okay, but the more I use it the better.

> I find the library much easier to use now and use it regularly for reference work I am studying.

They enjoyed access to computers, Prestel, interactive video, a telephone, newspapers, journals, photocopying and binding facilities as well as to books.

> It compares well with other libraries, having a computer, video and photocopier, all of which come in useful for doing work and getting projects in on time.
>
> (Student)

When Elaine came to the sixth form centre she changed the way the library was used – from a silent room to an area where working noise was allowed. This was an innovation which caused anxiety for some students and staff alike. Eventually a separate room was set aside for silent study so students with different learning preferences could be catered for, and also to provide more space. Staff anxieties were gradually overcome as Elaine worked closely and successfully with a number of departments. Students' borrowing of books increased for leisure as well as study.

Students have increasingly used the library and indeed on each field visit it was bursting at the seams. They used the wide range of resources available. In the first instance some students had to be helped by Elaine, or subject teachers, to formulate questions as they struggled to focus their research more sharply. Students then shared their new-found skills with their peers. Students following GCSE courses appeared to need more support from adults than those following A-level courses but:

> Following GCSE the word "project" was anathema to all and other terms such as research and investigation needed to be substituted.
>
> (Vice principal)

She also notes:

> The loan rate, use of the library by classes for study, formal

use for research, and informal use have all increased considerably and are clear indicators of success. It is interesting how good practice spreads, not only among teachers but also among students. The library is becoming an active centre of learning and is stimulating new resource based approaches.

(Vice principal)

There was clear management support for the library and librarian. The principal was supportive. Elaine worked closely with the vice principal in charge of library/resources, whilst the other vice principal was studying student-centred learning as part of her in-service Master's degree and thus was interested in the role of the library and understood the concept of information skills.

Students too played an active role in the management of the library as there were two representatives from the Student Council on the library committee. These two students were in constant informal contact with the librarian. Elaine runs courses for staff on how to use the National Educational Resources Information Services (NERIS), she also ensures that new staff are familiar with what the library can offer. She involved staff in the drawing up of a library policy. The SLS is also supportive, arranging in-service education and training activities and support, project loans and running an appraisal system which is supportive and developmental.

The Business Studies department made good use of the library and made explicit use of information skills as a framework for student research. The GCSE Business Studies group had to complete a number of assignments for their GCSE assessment and used the library for research. The library-use sheet devised by Elaine and the Business Studies teacher, Bill Mason, was as shown in Diagram 11.

Diagram 11

LIBRARY

GCSE Business Studies   Our town as an area for
Coursework 2   industrial location

1. <u>General Management and Business Studies</u>

There are several books with good sections on factors in the choice of location. *For example*:

BEARDSHAW, J. The Organisation in Its Environment. Pitman, 1986.
HAMMOND, S. Business Studies. Longman, 1988.
LIVESEY, F. et al. The Organisation in Its Environment, Vol 1. Longman 1980.

2.   Browse through the *subject catalogue* under (town name) and (county) and follow up any relevant shelf numbers. White cards mean that there is a *topic folder* at that number, in the filing cabinet. Individual items in the topic folders may be stamped out for overnight use (hand in an ordinary library ticket). There is a single copy of each item marked REFERENCE ONLY for use in the library. If all of the lending copies are out, you may fill in a request form and we will stop the borrower from renewing that item. If you all leave it until the last minute, some of you will be disappointed. *Before you borrow anything from the topic folders, it would be extremely useful to browse thoroughly through the folders to see which ones are the most important.*

3.   <u>Some useful periodicals</u>

–   (name of county) Business Monthly. December 1985 – merits a *quick browse*, may be useful for examples or ideas. (Back copies kept at 338.6042.)
–   [Other examples given of articles specific to the town.]

4.   <u>Other useful sections</u>

–   British Geography 914.2. *For example* NIXON, B. British Isles. Bell and Hyman, 1987, p172f.
–   Production Economics 338. *For example* KEMP, R. People in the Industrial Landscape. Macdonald, 1987. [Other examples given.]

5.   –   photocopier, 4p per side (pay at desk).
       –   binding (optional) Red or Blue Boards and Red or Blue Plastic Spiral costs 30p. Ask at desk.

Before students started on the assignment they had also been given a task to do in the library using a software package "Iron and Steel Location".

The students thus have a clear background to the concept they are exploring, an idea where to go in the library and how to go about getting the resources they need. Bill has provided the students with a clear outline of what he and the Examination Board expect of each student (see Diagram 12).

Diagram 12

GCSE BUSINESS STUDIES: COURSEWORK 2

(TOWN NAME) AS AN AREA FOR INDUSTRIAL LOCATION

Start: Monday 27 November
Due in: Friday 15 December

For this piece of coursework you have to present a report, and produce a brochure, designed to attract industry into the (town name) area.

The brochure should be interesting and informative and stress the positive aspects of locating a business in (town name).

The report should assess the factors which may deter firms from locating in the area.

Suggested Outline

1. Introduction: Explain the general ideas and factors which influence the location of industry.

2. Brochure: This should explain the particular advantage of (town name) as a site, and should include relevant data to support your case.

3. Disadvantages of the area: In this section you should explain the problems associated with (town name) as a location for industry, and again you should use relevant data.

4. Conclusion: Assess the relative importance of the various factors you have covered.

He gave each of the students a marking scheme (see Diagram 13).

The students found such an explicit marking scheme very helpful:

> It's invaluable. You could do a really good piece of work, but not get the marks if you didn't know.

Diagram 13

Marking

As can be seen from the scheme, there are 30 marks available. To score highly you must ensure that your report covers all five areas outlined. If you fail to show an understanding of all five areas your total mark will be low, no matter how well you do particular parts of the coursework.

MARKING SCHEME

NAME TUTOR GROUP	MAXIMUM MARK	ACTUAL MARK
1. The aim of the course work is understood including relevant facts, principles, terms or ideas.	10	
2. Appropriate information is selected for the coursework	5	
3. Information is presented accurately, logically and effectively	4	
4. Data has been analysed in written, numerical or graphical form	5	
5. Reasoned conclusions have been presented	6	
Total	30	

It was apparent that these students needed a framework or outline to work from. We asked if they had a plan of action:

> I haven't really thought about it – there's such a work overload that I haven't thought about the project till now. '

> There's so much information but it's the sort of subject it's hard to get started on.

> If I know well in advance what I'm expected to do I can deal with the workload and have time to do other things. I can read round the subject more.

> I spend a lot of time doing homework at night, including researching topics, but I never know how much extra I should do. No one really makes it clear.

The Business Studies teacher used a range of teaching strategies – whole-class teaching or discussion, small-group discussion and individual work.

Whilst students were working in the library on their GCSE assignment they were able to turn to the teacher or librarian for guidance. They discussed work with their peers, or worked alone.

During the period of the fieldwork one of the teachers at Poppy was conducting a piece of research for a Master's degree. The subject of her research was "Independence in the sixth" and she interviewed a number of students. There was a divergence of views over the role of the teacher. Some students felt that they needed teacher direction, others felt they wanted more freedom. For example one said:

> I like the way we are encouraged to find out for ourselves; it's better to learn for yourself, discover new relevant things along the way. One thing can often lead to another. By doing this you feel far less restricted.
>
> (De'Ath 1989)

Those who lacked confidence were still over-reliant on teacher notes and direction. These students read in an instrumental way, preferring their textbook in their desire for one view of a topic rather than coping with differing views. They were overly reliant on the teacher and preferred to be given notes which were "right". This reflects Stenhouse's view (1984) – "emancipation is potentially a matter of conflict in the sixth form, and largely because of the growth of independent study and the student's capacity to appeal against the teacher to the library". These students were not ready to accept that there might be alternative views of knowledge.

The majority of students interviewed by the vice principal during the course of her degree study valued class discussion:

> Teaching is good in the respect that it is not "come in and sit down, books out, teacher talk, end". There is a lot of open discussion which involves the whole group, there is a chance for you to develop ideas and opinions and let them be known which helps you to get to know others in your group, and helps the teacher to know you better which makes the atmosphere more relaxed and friendly, but you can still learn at the same time.

They preferred to think for themselves:

> If you ask a teacher a question, they don't give you a direct answer but instead ask you questions around the topic so you can answer your own problem yourself.
>
> (De'Ath 1989)

Those who were less confident preferred small-group discussion and were aware that if they could only participate more they would gain.

As far as essay writing was concerned there were mixed feelings about its value. Some felt it an inefficient way of learning whilst others felt it gave you an idea of style and how well you knew your subject. They felt preparation for essays was vital and that thinking through ideas, followed by discussion, then by writing was a good way forward. A number expressed the view that they would like more guidance on the depth and content required of them in an essay.

Their preferred teaching style was lively, being treated as adults, being able to use their initiative, group work, discussion and the teacher listening to their points of view. Getting the balance right between too much teacher direction and not enough guidance and support is problematic. This issue is one which faces many teachers when dealing with GCSE and its assignments (see DES 1988b, 1988c).

The librarian in this sixth form centre was committed to independent study. She had the support of the senior management team and the SLS. She worked with individual teachers to incorporate explicit

81

information skills teaching into their subject areas, and worked alongside students and staff in the library when appropriate. She ran in-service courses for staff at the sixth form centre. Staff at the centre used a range of teaching strategies to support their students. The librarian gained feedback on her performance from staff, students (through the library committee and individually) and through her appraisal with the SLS representative and the principal. She gained extra resources through negotiation with subject departments and an extra room for students to use for quiet study.

Summary

Students each have different preferred learning styles. Therefore, teachers have to employ a range of teaching strategies to develop individuals and help each student to reach their full potential.

Clear guidance on how to prepare for and research for assignments, together with explicit marking or assessment criteria are vital for students. This guidance has to be flexible to leave room for individual students' learning styles.

Students have to be encouraged to reflect on their own process of learning. As Carl Rogers put it:

> Learning is facilitated when the student participates responsibly in the learning process. When he chooses his own direction, helps to discover his own learning resources, formulates his own problems, decides his own course of action, lives with the consequences of each of these choices, then significant learning is maximised.
>
> Independence, creativity, and self-reliance are all facilitated when self-criticism and self-evaluation are basic...
> (Rogers 1969)

In each of the examples we give, the librarian has worked closely with subject teachers and students.

6 Conclusions and Recommendations

GCSE calls for students to have sophisticated information skills. This applies to most subjects, irrespective of which Examination Board the subject or school follows. Students need access to a wide range of resources to back up their GCSE work. The school librarian has a key role to play in supporting students and teachers in GCSE assignment planning.

In this chapter the implications of this general conclusion are summarised in three sections: more specific conclusions, an implementation framework, and recommendations.

Conclusions

1. Schools are gradually building up their awareness of the need for students to have a clear framework of skills such as those outlined in the nine question steps by the Schools Council and British Library Working Party led by Marland (Marland (ed) 1981). This movement has been reinforced by the explicit skills statements made by the Examination Boards in their outlines of GCSE criteria and assessment objectives for each subject area. Similarly, the National Curriculum Council has sent out explicit skills statements emphasising information skills (see Chapter 1 for examples).

2. Those schools without a long history of information skills teaching have found that they needed to emphasise information skills in Year 10 as their students begin to cope with GCSE assignments. However, schools are increasingly beginning such work lower in the school as they have come to appreciate that the skills are incremental, and that students need a sound base upon which to build. The National Curriculum will continue the momentum. Inevitably, past omissions have meant that much work is having to be done at Year 10 level to initiate students into this way of working in order for them to fulfil the requirements of GCSE.

3. Furthermore, some of the schools we visited were examining the idea of progression from primary to secondary, as well as from Year 7 to Year 11. They were attempting to draw up skills profiles to show what pupils had achieved in primary schools. This was in order that the secondary school could build upon

their work from Year 7 onwards. This is a feature which we did not see in our 1985-87 TVEI research. It would seem that the advent of the National Curriculum has also provided the impetus for better liaison between primary and secondary schools.

4. Nevertheless, the picture overall remains more pessimistic. The questionnaire returns from the LEAs and SLS, though limited in number, indicate that examples of interesting practice in information skills and GCSE are not widespread.

5. Those examples of good practice that we found are mainly in LEAs where there is an SLS and Advisory Service actively involved in supporting teachers, school librarians and schools in their implementation of information skills. This support has been in the form of close liaison between the SLS and Education Service and between those services and the schools. In-service education and training has been supported at the LEA-wide level and promoted within the school in the form of school-based in-service education and training.

6. The status and involvement of the school librarian have also been key factors. Those we have seen working towards whole-school approaches to information skills have been chartered librarians with head of department status. Alternatively, the person in charge of the library has been a senior teacher playing an active role in information skills teaching. The librarian has been actively involved in curriculum planning and development. They have been pro-active in both initiating and supporting developments in GCSE and information skills. They have urged schools to create a central resource area which consists of a range of resources to support students in GCSE assignment work. In in-service education and training activities they have been both a participant and a leader.

7. In those schools moving towards a more integrated approach to information skills, the senior management teams within the schools have given active support for the initiative. Where this has not happened, the librarian is left in isolation with only a small number of departments to influence. To instigate a whole-school approach to information skills, the management and organisational structures of the school may need to change, and it is only the head who can facilitate this.

8. Similarly schools and LEAs need to take account of the change process and employ an implementation strategy. This is discussed in more detail in the following section.

Implementation Framework

The factors associated with the successful implementation of information skills are the same as for any innovation. They are sixfold (see
Fullan and Park 1981):

1. **The characteristics of the innovation itself** – heads, teachers and
    librarians have to see the need for change. It has to be tied to the
    needs of the teacher in the classroom or library. The innovation
    has to be clearly articulated; the users need a clear, well struc-
    tured model and process. The need for all students to conduct
    research for GCSE assignments has created a universal need, but
    there remains a lack of clarity about the terms "information
    skills" or "study skills".

2. **The characteristics at LEA level** – there needs to be an established
    information skills policy. The Heeks report (1990) indicates that
    in her SLS questionnaire returns (some 85% responded from all
    SLS in the UK) the SLS reported that whilst 31% already had a
    policy on school libraries, a further 19 authorities are in the
    process of preparing them. It seems that the 1988 Education
    Reform Act is the motivator here. Furthermore, resources have
    to be made available; both financial and human. However,
    though many schools received capitation increases for GCSE
    which may or may not have been used to enhance the library or
    resource-based learning, few SLS received extra funding (only
    20% of the SLS received additional GCSE funding).

3. **The characteristics at the school level** – the culture of the school,
    the ability of its personnel to work collaboratively and the ability
    to plan and act are important features for success. The school
    needs support from parents, governors and the community.
    Teachers need to feel able to try things out in a safe environment,
    and so do students.

4. **The characteristics and activities of the key people**, i.e. the head,
    teachers, librarians, governors and LEA officials.

5. **The characteristics of the external environment**, such as the
    availability of funding and external support. At present schools
    are faced with increasing demands from government initiatives
    which put pressures on both time and resources.

6. **The characteristics of the strategies for innovation** – the quality of
    in-service education and training, a system of monitoring and

feedback and an understanding of the process of change. Change involves anxiety and uncertainty in the early stages. Teachers and librarians therefore require continuing technical and psychological support.

Recommendations

We have drawn up a list of advice based on the research and recent literature on information skills and on educational change.

There needs to be clarity about the innovation with a shared understanding and vocabulary amongst all staff involved. Clear guidelines on key skills need to be given. The skills work should be written into the school development plan, the aims and policy of the school, and into each subject syllabus.

As change takes time and requires ongoing support, in-service training has to be available. This training should utilise a variety of training components: integrated theory, demonstration, practice, feedback and coaching. Teachers and librarians need structured time to talk to each other about curriculum and teaching matters and to facilitate teacher/librarian collaboration and coaching.

Each subject department has to take responsibility for developing learning skills and for using a variety of teaching strategies. Some flexibility in timetabling may be required to foster more student-centred activities. Assessment and reporting systems for students have to give credit for *progress* in learning skills as the process is important, and not just the product. Students themselves need to be encouraged to reflect on their own work and take responsibility for their own learning. There is some specific advice for the four major groups involved as seen in Diagram 14.

At the school level the **senior management team** need to give a clear lead and create a climate in which skills work is valued and students *and* staff can learn. The appointment of a coordinator helps to ensure skills progression and continuity, preventing omission or unnecessary overlap of skills. They need to involve as many as possible in the development of information skills, including gaining support from parents and governors. The library/librarian needs to be integrated in the curriculum of the school and adequate resources given to support the innovation as well as open access to a range of multi-media resources.

Teachers need to take responsibility for developing information skills and for using a variety of teaching strategies with their students. Collaboration with other departments, teachers, and the librarian is another key to success. When planning the curriculum due regard has to be given to how the students can be assessed on their progress in learning skills.

Librarians have an active role to play in supporting both students and teachers in developing learning skills. It is important to be involved in curriculum planning at the department and school level. A wide range of resources need to be made available and promoted to both teachers and students. Collaborating with as many teachers and departments as possible is essential.

A lead at **LEA level** in establishing an information skills policy is also vital if we are to see the integration of information skills in the secondary curriculum. The integration of the SLS and Education Service, the involvement of the Advisory Service in learning skills, the provision of in-service education and training and the encouragement of cross-curricular initiatives together with the setting up of networks of good practice will all add to the impetus of this work.

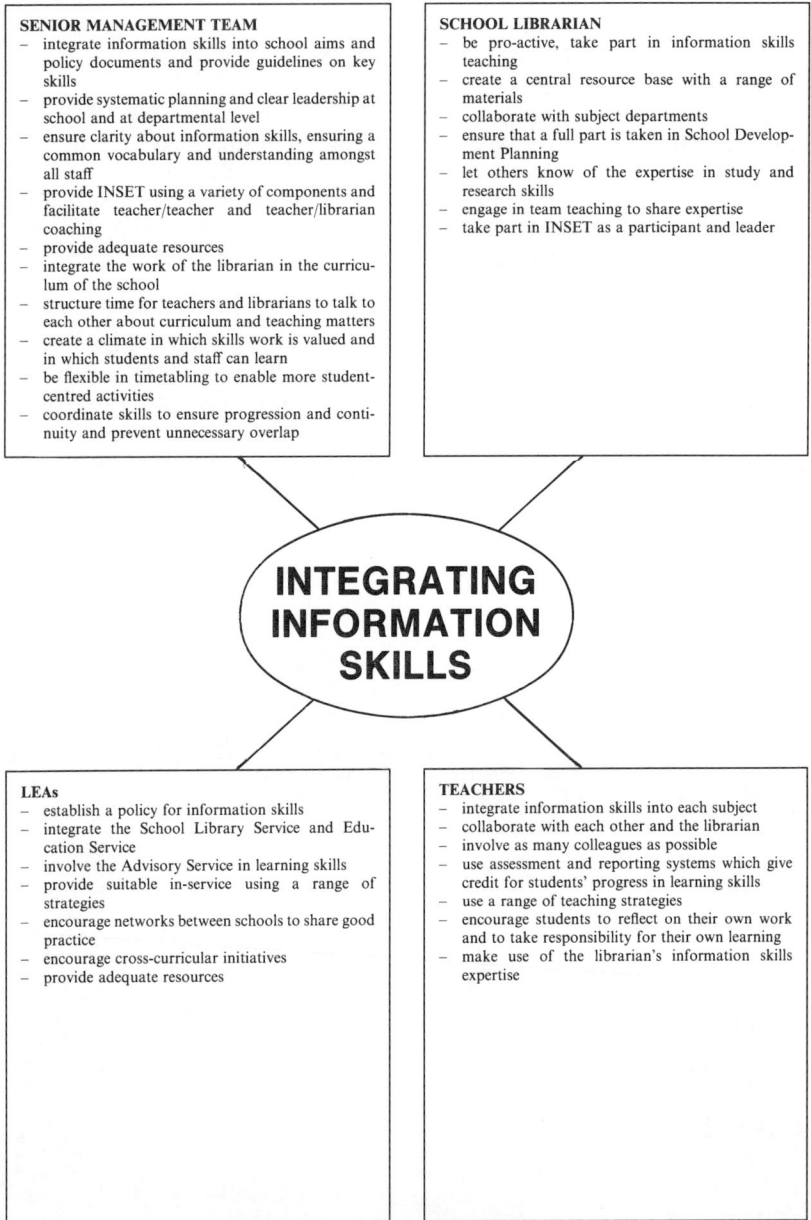

Diagram 14

SENIOR MANAGEMENT TEAM
- integrate information skills into school aims and policy documents and provide guidelines on key skills
- provide systematic planning and clear leadership at school and at departmental level
- ensure clarity about information skills, ensuring a common vocabulary and understanding amongst all staff
- provide INSET using a variety of components and facilitate teacher/teacher and teacher/librarian coaching
- provide adequate resources
- integrate the work of the librarian in the curriculum of the school
- structure time for teachers and librarians to talk to each other about curriculum and teaching matters
- create a climate in which skills work is valued and in which students and staff can learn
- be flexible in timetabling to enable more student-centred activities
- coordinate skills to ensure progression and continuity and prevent unnecessary overlap

SCHOOL LIBRARIAN
- be pro-active, take part in information skills teaching
- create a central resource base with a range of materials
- collaborate with subject departments
- ensure that a full part is taken in School Development Planning
- let others know of the expertise in study and research skills
- engage in team teaching to share expertise
- take part in INSET as a participant and leader

INTEGRATING INFORMATION SKILLS

LEAs
- establish a policy for information skills
- integrate the School Library Service and Education Service
- involve the Advisory Service in learning skills
- provide suitable in-service using a range of strategies
- encourage networks between schools to share good practice
- encourage cross-curricular initiatives
- provide adequate resources

TEACHERS
- integrate information skills into each subject
- collaborate with each other and the librarian
- involve as many colleagues as possible
- use assessment and reporting systems which give credit for students' progress in learning skills
- use a range of teaching strategies
- encourage students to reflect on their own work and to take responsibility for their own learning
- make use of the librarian's information skills expertise

Bibliography and References

BAILEY, A.J. (1987) *Support for School Management*. Beckenham: Croom Helm.

BATT, G. and SAGE, S. (1990) *He Obviously Had No Idea What He Was Doing*. Research and Development Report No. 12, Kent County Library Services.

BESWICK, N. (1988) A framework of possibilities. In Kinnell, M. and Pain-Lewins, H. (eds) *School Libraries and Curriculum Initiatives*, pp.30-41. British Library Research and Development Report 5969. London: Taylor Graham.

BOLAM, R. (1982) *Inservice Education and Training of Teachers: A Condition for Educational Change*. Paris: OECD.

BOLAM, R. (1987) *What is Effective INSET?* Paper addressed to Annual Members Conference of the National Foundation for Educational Research in England and Wales. December.

CAMBRIDGESHIRE COUNTY COUNCIL EDUCATION DEPARTMENT (1990) *Learning Now. The Cambridgeshire Experience in Science*. Cambridge: Cambridgeshire County Council.

CHRISTIAN-CARTER, J. and BURTON, J. (eds) (1988) *GCSE: A New Teaching Approach*. London: Council for Educational Technology.

DE'ATH, J. (1989) Independence in the sixth: a study of teaching, learning and the library. Unpublished thesis. University of East Anglia/Cambridge Institute of Education.

DES (1985) *Report by HM Inspectors on a Survey of Secondary School Libraries in Six Local Education Authorities*. London: DES.

DES (1986) Local Education Authority Training Grants Scheme: Financial Year 1987-88. Circular 6/86. London: HMSO.

DES (1988a) *Report by HM Inspectors on a Critique of the Implementation of the Cascade Model Used to Provide INSET for Teachers in Preparation for the Introduction of the General Certificate of Secondary Education*. London: DES.

DES (1988b) *A Report by HM Inspectors on GCSE: An Interim Report*. London: DES.

DES (1988c) *Report by HM Inspectors on the Introduction of the General Certificate of Education in Schools 1986-88*. London: DES.

DES (1989) *Better Libraries: Good Practice in Schools: A Survey by HM Inspectorate*. London: HMSO.

DES (1990a) *Report by HM Inspectors on the GCSE in Further Education*. London: DES.

DES (1990b) *Report by HM Inspectors on the GCSE in Schools and Sixth Form Colleges 1988-9*. London: DES.

DES (1990c) *A Survey of Secondary School Libraries in Six Local Education Authorities, September 1988-July 1989. A Report by HM Inspectorate.* London: DES.

DUNN, R. (1987) GCSE will benefit all. *SEC News.* No.7, pp.2-3.

FULLAN, M. (1982) *The Meaning of Educational Change.* New York: Teacher Educational Press.

FULLAN, M. (1985) Change processes and strategies at the local level. *The Elementary School Journal.* Vol.85, No.5, pp.391-421.

FULLAN, M. and PARK, P. (1981) *Curriculum Implementation.* Ontario: Ministry of Education.

GCSE NETWORK PROJECT (1989) *GCSE: A Positive Experience.* Tunbridge Wells: AEB.

HEEKS, P. (1989) *Perspectives on a Partnership: Information Skills and School Libraries 1983-88.* British Library Research Review 13. London: British Library.

HEEKS, P. (1990) *School Library Services Today.* British Library Research and Development Report 6024. London: British Library.

HOPKINS, D. (1986) The change process and leadership in schools. *School Organization,* Vol.6, No.1, pp.81-100.

HOPKINS, D. (ed) (1986) *Inservice Training and Educational Development.* London: Croom Helm.

HOPKINS, D. (ed) (1987) *Knowledge, Information Skills and the Curriculum.* Library and Information Research Report 46. London: British Library.

HOUNSELL, D. and MARTIN, E. (1983) *Developing Information Skills in Schools: A Dissemination Project.* Library and Information Research Report 9. London: British Library.

HOWARD, J. and HOPKINS, D. (1988) *Information Skills in TVEI and the Role of the Librarian.* British Library Research Paper 51. London: British Library.

HOWARD, J. and HOPKINS, D. (1990) *Crossing the Great Divide: With Support the School Librarian Can Enhance Pupils' Learning.* British Library Research and Development Report 6014. London: British Library.

JOYCE, B. and SHOWERS, B. (1988) *Student Achievement Through Staff Development.* New York; London: Longman.

KINNELL, M. and PAIN-LEWINS, H. (eds) (1988) *School Libraries and Curriculum Initiatives.* British Library Research and Development Report 5969. London: Taylor Graham.

LIBRARY AND INFORMATION SERVICES COUNCIL (SCOTLAND) (1985) *Library Services and Resources for Schools in Scotland.* London: HMSO.

LIBRARY AND INFORMATION SERVICES COUNCIL WORKING PARTY ON SCHOOL LIBRARY SERVICES (1984) *School Libraries: The Foundations of the Curriculum.* London: HMSO.

LIBRARY ASSOCIATION (1977) *Library Resource Provision in Schools: Guidelines and Recommendations.* London: Library Association.

LIBRARY ASSOCIATION (1988) *General Certificate of Secondary Education: Guidance Note on the Role of Libraries and Librarians.* London: Library Association.

LINCOLN, P. (1987) *The Learning School.* Library and Information Research Report 62. London: British Library.

LONDON AND EAST ANGLIAN GROUP (1987) Underway with GCSE Geography. London: LEAG.

MARKLESS, S. (1986) Towards an information skills network. *School Librarian.* Vol.34, No.1, pp.21-25.

MARKLESS, S. and LINCOLN, P. (eds) (1986) *Tools for Learning.* British Library Research and Development Report 5892. London: British Library.

MARLAND, M. (ed) (1981) *Information Skills in the Secondary Curriculum.* Schools Council Curriculum Bulletin 9. London: Methuen.

NATIONAL CURRICULUM COUNCIL (1990) Geography 5-16 in the National Curriculum. York: NCC.

NISBET, J. and SHUCKSMITH, J. (1986) *Learning Strategies.* London: Routledge & Kegan Paul.

PAIN, H. (1988) Project work & GCSE: can public libraries meet the challenge? *Public Library Journal.* Vol. 3, No. 3, pp.59-61.

PAIN-LEWINS, H. et al (1989) *Resourcing GCSE.* British Library Research Paper 58. London: British Library.

ROGERS, C.R. (1969) *Freedom to Learn.* Columbus, Ohio: Merrill.

RUDDUCK, J. (1981) *Making the Most of the Short Inservice Course.* Schools Council Working Paper 71. London: Methuen.

RUDDUCK, J. and HOPKINS, D. (1984) *The Sixth Form and Libraries: Problems of Access to Knowledge.* Library and Information Research Report 24. London: British Library.

SMITH, M. et al (eds) (1988) *Provision of Learning Resources in Secondary Schools.* Cambridge: Cambridgeshire County Council, Education Service.

STENHOUSE, L. (1984) in Rudduck, J. and Hopkins, D., op. cit.

TABBERER, R. (1987) *Study and Information Skills in Schools.* British Library Research and Development Report 5870. London: NFER-Nelson.

THOMSON, L. and MEEK, M. (1985) *Developing Resource Based Learning: One School's Approach.* York: Longman.

WALLACE, M. (1988) *Towards Effective Management Training Provision.* Bristol: National Development Centre for School Management Training.

Appendix 1

Questionnaire to Schools Library Services

1. Was extra funding made available at LEA level to
    support school libraries in GCSE provision?   YES/NO
    If yes – how much overall/per institution?

2. Was the School Library Service involved in training
    for GCSE introduction?   YES/NO
    If yes, please give details:

3. Have there been any direct links between the
    Examination Boards and the School Library Service
    with regard to GCSE?   YES/NO
    If yes, please give details:

4. Do school librarians receive ongoing in-service support at LEA
    or school level for their information skills work in GCSE?

5. Please give details of any examples of materials which have been
    especially developed for information skills in GCSE.

6. Have you any examples of schools/librarians who are carrying out cross-curricular initiatives in information skills teaching for GCSE? YES/NO
If yes, please outline some of the work they are undertaking:

7. Can you give details of any school or librarian whom we could contact for possible inclusion in our studies of interesting practice?

8. Is there a member of the LEA Advisory staff or other LEA officer who would be a useful contact in your Education Authority?

9. Do you have any further details you would like to add about information skills in GCSE?

Appendix 2

Violet School Library Resource Centre

ANALYSIS OF CLASS VISITS: Sept-Dec 1989
34 teachers brought classes to the library: 368 classes

Subject	Classes	Year 7	Year 8	Year 9	Year 10	Year 11
Science	138	37	7	15	40	39
English	118	63	29	15	7	4
Ch. Development	18				15	3
Art	17			1	6	10
Modern Languages	11		8	3		
Drama	9	7	1	1		
Social Science	28				26	2
Geography	5		2		1	2
History	2			2		
PSE	22	22				
TOTALS	368	129	47	37	95	60

ANALYSIS OF PUPILS WITH PERMISSION SLIPS: 5 March - 4 May 1990
Of 85 teaching staff 66 referred pupils for research in the library during the seven weeks surveyed.

Subject	Classes	Year 7	Year 8	Year 9	Year 10	Year 11
Social Science	16				8	8
Music	3				3	
Maths	53		15	6	14	18
English	413	104	51	144	50	64
Science	160			112	21	27
Modern Languages	171	4	7	149		11
History	309	73	44	62	83	47
Geography	115		13	11	70	21
Home Economics	48	2	9		12	25
Design	101	4	2	11	32	52
Special Needs	*16		5	4	1	6
PE	27	14	2	4	1	6
Art	299	8	7	36	52	196
Pottery						
Drama	5				2	3
TOTALS	1736	209	155	539	349	484

*Plus groups not recorded

Average of 50 pupils per day referred with permission slips.

Average no. of classes per day	5.5	=	138 pupils
Average no. per break	30×2	=	60 pupils
Average no. per lunchtime	60	=	60 pupils
Average no. with pupil permission slips	50	=	50 pupils

Average no. of pupils using library per day   308 pupils

PERMISSION SLIPS

Examples of type of research for which pupils are sent to library

Geography	Pollution. To check weather forecasts in daily newspapers. Rain forests.
Design	Projects for GCSE: e.g. designing clocks.
English	Choosing private reading books, evidence for discursive essays: e.g. animal rights, Channel tunnel, drugs.
Mod. Langs.	Language projects on various countries, languages.
History	Local history – finding evidence about local cholera outbreak. Information about Alfred the Great. Seventh-year pupils to find dates, etc. and compare notes about what they had found out. Local history – work on Castle project.
RE	Year 9 pupils each had to prepare a lesson for other pupils on different religions and festivals.
Art	Preparation for GCSE examinations – looking for background on artists to set their work in context. Source material for compositions, photographs, etc.
Home Econ.	Herbs and spices.
Science	Find information on acids and alkalis. Predictions and statistics.

Appendix 3

VIOLET SCHOOL GEOGRAPHY DEPARTMENT

1. Presenting your Coursework

TITLE PAGE

CONTENTS PAGE

INTRODUCTION: Aim or hypothesis. The PURPOSE of your investigation.

DATA COLLECTION: Explain what data was collected; how it was collected. What problems did you have?

PRESENTATION OF DATA: Use a variety of techniques. Maps, diagrams, graphs of various types, photos, sketches...

WRITE UP and INTERPRET the data or findings:
Describe what the graphs etc. show.
Analyse them.
What have you discovered as a result of your investigation?
Can you give/explain reasons for your findings?
Include your own observations/thoughts/ideas/views.

CONCLUSIONS: Restate aim/purpose of investigation.
Briefly explain how/what data collected.
What has your work shown?
Summarise your findings.
Have you achieved your aim?

BIBLIOGRAPHY: Sources of information.

Advice

1. You can collect data in a group to save time but work has to be written up individually.
2. Any questionnaires devised need to be short. I need to check them to see if they are suitable. Be polite when talking to people. Interview in pairs.
3. Quality is more important than quantity. Take account of suggested word limit.

4. Good presentation is vital. Use your imagination. Diagrams, maps, etc. should be presented on plain paper, not lined.
5. Organise your investigation logically. Integrate written text with diagrammatic material. Refer to all diagrams, graphs, maps in the text.
6. Explain findings. Do not simply describe.
7. Originality is important: do not copy chunks from books. Make use of personal observation.
8. Organise your time: stick to deadlines.

2. Geographical Enquiry: Guidance Notes

Step 1: Choose a Topic
Try to identify some particular issue or problem to investigate. Your teacher will help in the choice of a suitable topic. It must be geographical. The best topics to study are often those which are "local" and accessible to you. Your enquiry must not be too general. Limit your enquiry to a topic which you can research thoroughly in the time available.

Step 2: Decide on the Wording of the Aim or Hypothesis
· An aim is a brief description of the topic to be investigated. It does not give any hint of the final conclusion. Aims should begin with the word **to**. E.g. "**To** compare two shopping areas".
· Hypothesis. This is a statement which the study is designed to either prove or disprove. A hypothesis is like an idea. Hypotheses should begin with the word **that**. E.g. "**That** industry on Weasenham Lane is closely related to farming".
Think about your aim or hypothesis carefully.

Step 3: Decide on Methods
· What data or information are you going to collect?
· How are you going to collect it? What equipment is required?
· How are you going to process and present the information? (Maps, diagrams, graphs, photographs, tape recordings, written analysis.) Try to use a variety of techniques and use your imagination! Try to be original.

Step 4: Collecting Data/Information. The Fieldwork Part
· Collect only relevant data.
· Collect enough data to make reasoned judgements.
· Data can be collected in groups but final analysis must be your own.
· Secondary sources (e.g. textbooks) can be used to support your investigations, but take care. Your own research should provide the bulk of the information you need.
· Care is needed in wording questionnaires – ask your geography teacher.

- Be polite to people when doing questionnaire type work.
- Safety is important, especially in busy urban areas.
- Wear suitable clothing.

Step 5: Presenting and Interpreting (Analysing) Your Findings/Results
- Be neat; take care with layout/appearance. Do not cram too much onto a page (paper is free!). Do not write a whole page without any sub-headings/paragraphs. Type if you wish. Use good English and do not cross anything out. Number the pages. The presentation should put the examiner in a good mood before he/she starts to read your study in detail. Print on maps and use colour (take care with felts). All maps, diagrams, graphs etc. must have a title, key, etc. Scale and compass direction on all maps. Annotate if necessary, especially sketches/photographs. Underline important statements in any article/newspaper cuttings included. This shows you have read and thought about them.

- All data needs to be interpreted and analysed. Describe your findings carefully. Describe maps, results and graphs etc. Draw attention to important points. The text (written part) should be fully integrated with maps/graphs etc.
- Suggest reasons for your results – often difficult but vital. Ask for help.
- Be precise, concise and "to the point".

Step 6: Conclusions
- Draw conclusions throughout, not just at the end.
- The overall conclusion should be concise and answer the aim or hypothesis set. Re-read your aim or hypothesis before writing the overall (final) conclusion.
- Your final conclusion should re-state the original aim and then highlight the findings.
- Include your own views/ideas but justify them.
- Your conclusion is vital and heavily weighted in terms of marks awarded.
- Add a bibliography if needed (sources of information).
- Appendices may be appropriate.

Other Points
- Remember **QUALITY** is more important than **QUANTITY**. A concise enquiry, based mainly on original first-hand research presented well will gain more marks than a long, generalised study where much has been copied from textbooks.
- Stick to deadlines.
- Present your enquiry in a good quality folder – you get it back!

· If you have any problems – see your geography teacher (in good time!).

3. Guidance for Pupils

<u>Geographical Enquiry – Stage 1</u>

Name: _____ Teacher: _____

1. Provisional Title (What idea/hypothesis do you intend to test?):

_____

_____

_____

2. Brief statement of what you think you will include in your work:

_____

_____

_____

3. METHOD. How do you intend to carry out your work?

_____

_____

_____

4. What TECHNIQUES do you intend to use?

_____

_____

_____

5. What RESOURCES will you need? (Maps? Reference Books? Fieldwork equipment? etc.)

_____

_____

_____

Other reports

Library and Information Research (LIR) Reports may be purchased from the British Library Publications Sales Unit, Boston Spa, Wetherby, West Yorkshire LS23 7BQ UK. Details of some other LIR Reports are given below.

LIR Report 76. Tuck, Bill, Archer, David, Hayet, Marie and McKnight, Cliff. *Project Quartet*. 1990. pp 275. ISBN 0 7123 3207 3.

The traditional method of information exchange in research communities involves the production, review, distribution and study of scholarly documents. As electronic communication, storage and display technologies have advanced, new opportunities to improve information exchange have arisen. Research workers can now call on teleconferencing facilities, write papers on word processors and view A4 pages on screens. Project Quartet has examined many of these technologies and applied them to a variety of situations. This is the main report on Quartet, a $3\frac{1}{2}$ year research programme which ended in June 1989, carried out by the universities of Birmingham and Loughborough, Hatfield Polytechnic and University College London, with advice from the International Electronic Publishing Research Centre. The report provides an opportunity to find out more about the limitations of current methods for carrying out many research-orientated tasks and Quartet's solutions to them.

LIR Report 77. Miles, Ian and contributors. *Mapping and measuring the information economy*. 1990. pp. 285. ISBN 0 7123 3212 X.

This is a detailed critical guide to data and data sources which depict the development, in the UK, of activities involving new information technology. Proposals are made concerning both the better utilisation of existing statistical material, and the sorts of changes that are required if we are to get a better grasp of patterns of social and economic change around the information economy. The report draws upon studies undertaken by a group of researchers at the Science Policy Research Unit, Sussex University. It is the first attempt to provide an overview and route-map to the empirical material on this broad set of topics, and provides a marked contrast to the provocative but speculative visions, and rich but restricted case-studies, which constitute so much of the literature on the "information economy".

LIR Report 78. Best, Ron, Abbott, Fiona and Taylor, Mike. *Teaching skills for learning: information skills in teacher education.* 1990. pp 137. ISBN 0 7123 3213 8.

There is a growing body of research to suggest that the pupils in primary and secondary schools are not encouraged to use the library, nor provided with much opportunity to do so. References to libraries and resource centres as the "hub" of the curriculum appear to have largely a rhetorical force. The teaching of study skills, library skills and the handling of information generally seems to be given low priority in many schools. The research reported here begins with the hypothesis that these deficiencies are at least partly the result of the way teachers are trained. Using interviews, observation and questionnaires, the report explores the place of the library and of information-handling skills in the BEd courses offered in four teacher-training institutions. Attention is focused on the important issues of assessment, the integration of study skills, library use and course content, and the impact of emotional factors on library use, and some examples of good practice are offered. The report concludes with an agenda of issues for debate by all those involved in the review and development of teacher-training courses.

LIR Report 79. Squirrell, Gillian, Gilroy, Peter, Jones, David and Rudduck, Jean. *Acquiring knowledge in initial teacher education: reading, writing, practice and the PGCE course.* 1990. pp 102. ISBN 0 7123 3216 2.

This study focuses on the contribution of reading and writing, libraries and resource centres, and teaching practice to the development of a would-be teacher's professional knowledge. It examines PGCE courses in six universities and the perceptions of staff and students of the purpose of the course. The report describes and analyses the students' conceptions of reading and writing as part of their training, and their use of university and departmental libraries. It uncovers tensions in the design and rhythm of PGCE courses and in the contributions to students' training of university- and school-based experience.

LIR Report 80. Irving, Ann. *Wider horizons: online information services in schools.* 1990. pp 150. ISBN 0 7123 3224 3.

An investigation was undertaken in six schools, one primary and five secondary, into the educational value and use of online information services. The schools worked for six terms using a range of datafiles from a selection of UK and overseas online hosts. Development, progress and results were monitored by means of observations, interviews, and diaries kept by school staff. Regular meetings were held to develop staff expertise and to share their experiences. The online host companies provided access to their services for the duration of the project, usually free of charge. Teachers were encouraged to explore relevant files for a range of curricular topics in geography, history, religious education, science and modern languages. The value of online services in schools arises from the nature of the modern school curriculum. This emphasises the development of information-handling skills, the use of a wide range of information sources, the need for very topical information and for an understanding of how new information technologies are being applied. Recommendations are made for online host companies, teachers, librarians, school management, training organisations, research and professional bodies.

LIR Report 81. Orminski, Evelyn M. *Business information needs of science park companies.* 1991. pp 118. ISBN 0 7123 3246 4.

This report investigates the business information needs of science park companies and examines the application of these findings to an information service set up within the Aston Science Park. It goes on to discuss the results from monitoring the first six months of the information service and draws out the implications for its future operations. The key finding of the report is the relationship between business and information strategies, such that those companies without a coherent business strategy were found to have little interest in information. This finding has major implications for information specialists who are seen to require an understanding of business and a proactive approach to marketing and information education. Consideration is given to the way in which an information service could successfully operate and market its services within a science park environment. The report concludes with recommendations for motivating companies to develop business plans, the setting-up of information services to businesses, charging levels, the development of artificial intelligence tools for information strategies, further EC-wide research, and the benefits to science parks generally.

LIR Report 82. Erens, Bob. *Research libraries in transition: academic perceptions of recent developments in university and polytechnic libraries.* 1991. pp 210. ISBN 0 7123 3247 2.

This report presents the results of a large-scale survey of over 2000 UK academics. The main objective of the survey was to examine the importance for academic research of university and polytechnic libraries and how well these libraries meet research needs. The survey also examined the researchers' perceptions of recent developments in library collections and services and the possible consequences for academic research of those developments. There is evidence that many academics' needs are not being met by their libraries' collections; compared with five years ago, there is more use of inter-library loan and of personal purchase of items. There is more use of photocopied material and less reliance on browsing. On the positive side, there is easier access to a wider range of bibliographic information. Nearly half of the respondents suggested that improvements to collections were needed.